THE RELUCTANT JIHADIST:
SMOKE FROM THE MACHINE

BY

UMAR A. HASSAN

BLACKHORSE & LONGMOON PUBLISHING

1500 NORTH AVENUE 50

LOS ANGELES, CALIFORNIA 90042

2006© BY UMAR A. HASSAN

NOVEMBER 2006

ISBN 978-0-6151-3621-9

DEDICATED TO

TIJANI IBRAHIM & ALIYA ESTCLAR

HANDLE WITH CARE

I used the interview as a subterfuge for revealing an interior dialog. The conundrum was determining, when questioning my own views, what was a challenging question as opposed to sycophancy. I was surprised how difficult it was to answer my own questions without resorting to pat faith statements that I had never challenged with any real objective intent. When examining my responses to my questions, it was chilling to be exposed, especially by myself, as irrational on so many points. These points, some of which I left just as they first were uttered, are not irrational in the sense of being spiritual or mystical; rather, they were posed as logical and they were not.

The fact that the subject is religious belief makes illogic bearable in the minds of some. However, these are the same minds that hold the concept of god walking through the Garden of Eden genuinely searching for his creatures, Adam and his boney wife Eve, who have evidently gone missing and, at the same time, imagine and build a space-based telescope capable of taking incredible photographs of galaxies, planets, stars, and transmitting them back to us on earth – all in the same mind.

I wanted, moreover, to tell how it feels to be an African American Muslim who still has serious faith questions and enjoys the process of trying to resolve them, as painful as it is. It is self-examination, along with the published blogs, in which I try to explain myself and describe how I am sometimes consistent with that explanation, as dynamic as it is. Sometimes I fail to meet the behavioral standards I accepted when I spoke the words of commitment to Islam. This contrariness, it isn't hypocrisy because I acknowledge the contradictions, is the reflection of an unapologetic leeriness of organizations based on mysteries shrouded in histories and an honest attempt to make sense of all of it with an admittedly secondary goal that others gain some personal insights through objectifying mine.

Each title of a poem followed with this symbol ◯ indicates that it was previously published in The Mulberry Blues that was published earlier this year.

FORWARD

The managing editor of BlackHorse & LongMoon Publishing is committed to creating opportunities for discussing contemporary issues in an extended, thoughtful format. Opportunity has many guises and one of them, the interview, offers the chance to see how one person organizes his psychosocial reality of being Muslim in the United States. When I was approached about participating in someway, I had not thought of it as a part of our agreement to publish selections from my blog. But after reviewing the first proofs of the interview, I saw its relation to the blogs I had already selected.

The interview addresses the history of Islam in America, international Islamic movements, Qur'anic interpretations, and, of course, jihad. The contextualization of these issues within the American milieu is revealing especially to those who have formed their responses to these challenges as if they were foreign, naturally alien to all things American. That is why an American was the perfect subject to challenge preconceptions that we necessarily formed in the culture of fear the American government created and maintained known as the war on terror.

I began posting on-line approximately three years ago when I finally succumbed to fashion. Many entries were extemporaneous although some were more carefully constructed. Usually, I would log on and begin writing about the first thing that came to mind. These entries ordinarily reflected the political headlines of that day or something that had been gestating for a week or so. It wasn't long before I realized that the news from the Middle East and my personal trials and tribulations seemed more important than anything else in the world.

There is a good reason why blogs are known as rants. In reading through my entries, I found that some were nothing more. Rarely did rants contain anything worth repeating and those that did have a saving grace often required extensive editing or rewriting. The more personal have been redacted more in the hope of hiding my pettiness than being merciful or forgiving to my subjects.

I've selected 99 of the more coherent posts. They are presented in chronological order. Later, I added headlines that coincided with the date of each post's entry date. Sometimes the headlines and the subject of the posts related eerily. In any event, they reminisce about events that are recent enough to shine light on the events of today revealing all kinds of cracks and flaws inherent in the government's foreign and domestic policies.

THE RELUCTANT JIHADIST

CONTENTS

PART I

INTERVIEW WITH THE RELUCTANT JIHADIST
PAGE 5

PART II

SMOKE FROM THE MACHINE
PAGE 33

THE RELUCTANT JIHADIST

The interviewee requested anonymity and we agreed reluctantly. He also previewed the manuscript and suggested clarifications, some to which we also agreed. We felt obligated to create pseudonyms for some of the people he mentioned during the interview because we did not have the resources required to check the facts thoroughly or to elicit responses from those mentioned or implicated.

The actual interview occurred over three days. While we were interrupted inadvertently each day, the majority of the text reflects the first day.

INTRODUCTION
Today, political pundits say we're witnessing a clash of civilizations. Western, Judeo-Christian civilization is being challenged for preeminence by Islamic civilization. Stateless, militant jihadists are attacking the United States of America, the leader of the Western world, its allies and their interests. Whether this is more than hyperbole, witness the horrendous acts of violence against the United States and its allies by these stateless jihadists.

Whether they represent a majority point of view in the Muslim world is moot, the question is how the Western world views the jihadists in relationship to the rest of the Muslim world. The media need to train their cameras and commentary on the most dramatic, plays to the false conclusion that many, if not most, Muslims support the jihadists.

The use of civilian airliners as weapons of mass destruction against the World Trade Center, a symbol of America's international hegemony, brought this clash into stark relief. We have, since then, become accustomed to the language of terror.

BLP: *The Western world versus the Islamic world is described euphemistically as the war on terrorism. Do they have it right?*

Do these propagandists have it right? Of course they don't. Your question suggests that you might not have it right either. These analyses are flawed on at least two counts. It is literally impossible, in the first place, to divide world into Western civilization and Islamic civilization.

Although the organizations that are fighting the United States and its allies are not formally associated with any states (they, in fact, have added a twist to the expression non-governmental organization or NGO), a roster of those known to have participated in attacks lists Saudis primarily. Egyptians are also represented. There have been attacks in Malaysia and Pakistan that may have been executed by indigenous jihadists.

Regardless, the fact is that the jihadists do not and cannot claim to be representing the points of view of very many Muslims. In fact, the jihadists express a need to reform the international Muslim community that, in their view, has gone astray. To generalize the motives of the jihadists to all Muslims is specious.

One would hope that the pundits would know by now that nearly 70 percent of the world's Muslims reside in Asia and nearly 30 percent reside in Africa. Every other place, including Saudi Arabia, has what amounts to loose change in the global percentiles.

Second point, how can there be a war against an abstraction? To declare war against abstractions seems a modern predilection of Americans. America has waged unsuccessful wars against poverty and drugs. You see, since the war is against something that has no oppositional reality, it can never be measured and therefore never won.

Some people get rich making wars but who gets rich making peace?

What we see today is less a clash of civilizations than it is a clash of those who have wealth and power and those who have not. Does anyone really believe that Muslims have as a goal the destruction of Western civilization? First, I cannot imagine Muslims agreeing on any goal even if it were specifically articulated in the Qur'an.

Muslims, I believe, want to be westernized. Muslims want high definition televisions, Mercedes Benzes, air-conditioned homes, Coca Cola; all the material goods the West sells. What the Wahhabis seem to want, on the other hand, is to live in a mythic although draconian caliphate. It is not about civilization. It is not simply about oil. It is, strictly observed, about power to.

When the neighborhood bully struts up to you and threatens to smash your face, take your money and your pride, there will either be a fight or surrender. Aggressive behavior is often reciprocated with violence. I propose to you that the Western world has provoked Muslims with all kinds of aggressions the intent being to not just control the natural resources of the Muslim world although that is a valued byproduct. The purpose is really the same as that storied bully's purpose. It is humiliation and domination to establish who will teach Muslim children. You should understand that. If the bully teaches the children, the children will follow the bully and speak like the bully and like all of the things the bully likes, hate all the things the bully hates. So, our children will hate us and necessarily hate themselves.

How can our children survive hating themselves?

BLP: *Is there a conspiracy among Western nations to dominate the Muslim world?*

No, there is no conspiracy in the sense that you mean it. The political and business leaders of the Western nations have not gotten together in the proverbial smoke filled room to decide the fate of the world. Such a scenario is possible just highly unlikely. What seems to me more likely is that there is a confluence of interests on certain critical points such as energy, food, and military power. These confluences merge like rivers merge into the sea. There is the surface appearance of collaboration and harmony but beneath the water's plane, it roils, eddies, and works things out just as the interests of international corporations and their surrogate nation-states forge agreements and make compromises.

BLP: *Elaborate your idea of confluence of interests.*

I don't know that this is originally my concept but I can explain what I mean with an example. An international plastics company relies on petrochemicals originating in Nation A. Nation A wants Nation B, which happens to be where the plastics company is headquartered, to lower its tariffs on petrochemicals. The company uses its economically based political muscle influencing the decision of Nation B. Nation B then asks that Nation A allow it to place an airbase in a secluded region of Nation A as a forward defense post allowing it to spy on Nations C, D, and E.

Once the airbase is operational and the international press learns of it, the story could be spun in different ways but the confluent interests of the company and Nation A to lower company A's petrochemical costs which in turn will increase demand is the primary cause in the chain of events culminating as an airbase controversy. The media may see the airbase as a staging area for joint military adventurism to control the price of petroleum. The media could also see it for what it is but the media cannot logically gore its masters' oxen.

Explode this example into a million transactions and the relationship between the Western World and the Muslim World, being a neighborhood in the Third World, becomes clearer. My "rivers to the sea" analogy rages on.

BLP: *What are the shared interests of the people of the Muslim world?*

When the media depict Muslims, they are generally Arabs. What if China regularly depicted Americans as Native Americans? The Muslim world actually outgrew its Arabness long ago. I think the Arabs come to the Westerner's mind for the obvious reasons: Islam was born in Arabia; the Qur'an is Arabic making the language of worship universally Arabic; and the two prominent religious sites are in Saudi Arabia. Other than that, there are no reasons. I know. I know. These are pretty compelling reasons. But embracing the relevant statistical data is like walking into a mosque in Malaysia on a Friday afternoon.

But these facts and artifacts have little relevance to the political interests of Malaysia. As diverse as the Muslim world has always been, even from its inception, Muslims have very few interests that they do not share with non-Muslims. For the most part, these interests have to do with a very limited number of business and personal transactions.

Muslims, and I shouldn't have to mention this, are not a monolith of ideas or beliefs. Nor are Muslims monolithic in their practice of their faith. In the same manner, Muslims even differ greatly on questions of political authority.

Muslims absorbed aspects of the cultures they encountered as Islam spread into Egypt, North and West Africa and into Italy, then to southern France. These advances were military to be sure but the Muslims brought more than arms, they brought the knowledge they were gathering from Africa, India and Greece. They turned on a bright, renascent light ending the Dark Ages. West Africa continued to bloom becoming the home of Islamic centers of learning.

They gave credit were credit was due. For example, Muslims called the numbers they learned from India, Hindi numbers. Today, the West calls them Arabic numbers because they learned the numbers from Muslims. The Indians spurred the development of a nascent Islamic mysticism. Sufis are very close to the profound esoteric knowledge that supports Indian culture.

And we can't forget Africa. The Africans contributed heavily to the history of Islam from the time of the prophet through the codification of Islamic law. The Maliki School is tied to Africans historically and practically.

Muslims came to the United States to enjoy its liberties and accumulate whatever wealth they could. This is what immigrants do. They did not come here to destroy America. They came here to exploit it, first as students and then as professionals. All you have to do is visit the mosques they constructed and you see most of the attendees who are either immigrants or the sons and daughters of immigrants as solidly middle class Americans.

In contrast, the disenfranchised African Americans brought their anger to their mosques. If I had been looking for militant Islam in America, I would have been looking seriously at the African American communities. Of course, I would have been wrong. Most of them were struggling with the legacies of poverty and disenfranchisement. When the African American Muslims experienced prejudice in these immigrant run mosques, for the most part they retreated to their mosques that were essentially an extension of the storefront church phenomenon common to African American Christian communities.

These mosques were more inward looking than anything else. The women, victimized by rampant polygyny, experienced the only noticeable terror. These women were often on welfare and the men often did not work. The stereotypical African American Muslim was an incense seller, garbed in stereotypical rural Arab clothes.

They were so inward looking that terrorism was not even an afterthought. Certainly, there was hatred expressed against America in these mosques but I believe these Muslims were so overwhelmed by their immediate circumstances that they feel powerless to even challenge the status quo publicly even with angry words.

BLP: *Do you connect slavery with the rise of Islam in America?*

Yes. You have to remember that many of the people captured and brought to the Americas were Muslims. The evidence is overwhelming. I'm not saying that there is a direct generational relationship between those captured Muslims and Muslims in America now but there are substrata in the cultural milieu of

African Americans that suggest more than a casual relationship between what social anthropologists categorize as African survivals and the representation of Islam here today.

African Americans are smart enough to have figured this out years ago. And, not unlike the current day Islamic romanticists pining away for that mythical caliphate, it is easy enough to draw straight lines through history to the time West Africa was dominated by Muslims.

Since Islam had been in the source areas of the slave trade for centuries, it is not surprising that we can point to firm evidence of African survivals in our culture. My ancestors for example, are noted for several behaviors that can be related to Islam. They did not drink alcohol or eat pork. The men gathered together on Thursday evenings to worship. These are not necessarily definitive but they are very suggestive of some African survivals. Probably Muslim. A historian even places an Arab in their company when they first entered Mexico.

BLP: *Amid all of this diversity, there is a great deal of tension between Muslims and the Western world. How do you explain it?*

This tension has existed for over a thousand years. Its complexity has bled into facile stereotypes that are almost hardwired in our respective societies. This is true whether we're talking about the Western world or the Muslim world. We are still fighting mop up actions from the crusades. Well, at least from WW I. Despite this, the fact that we, the media crazed, are bombarded with images and sounds of angry mobs doing stupid things does not mean that the Muslim world is enraged.

They were competitors. At the outset, the Muslims won. Then the West won. The Muslims hung around, confused, mystified really, by their failures. But Islam bound them together on some core beliefs and practices. Now those beliefs, enriched by many other beliefs, are like a Josephine cloak, uniquely and beautifully multicolored. But there is no single voice that can even pretend to speak for the

Muslims. And those voices Muslims do have are strangely coded. Even when we translate them, we do not understand their real meanings, the symbols are filtered through mindsets older than El-Cid.

I would hope that Americans, the primary targets of this verbicide, would figure it out. The neo-conservatives view the war on terror as a pre-Armageddon pre-emptive war against Islam. Although they were slow to pay attention, when they did, they did so through biblical eyes. For Jesus to return, they believe, the Jews have to hold Israel.

BLP: *What about terrorism?*

This very odd concept "war on terror" demonstrates the danger of verbicide. How can there be a war against a tactic? How can there be a state sanctioned war that has an indefinable enemy? The sleight of tongue is to confuse its own citizenry. Now, the enemy is the boogey man. He is hiding in the closets of our minds; cringing under our beds; lurking in the waiting areas of our airports; and he is necessarily the other which for Americans means he is brown or black and probably not a Christian.

Do you think that the Palestinians who have been living in tents since 1948 are the perpetrators or the victims of terror? I'm not pointing my finger at Israel. The Jews of Europe were victims of terror but nobody calls the Nazis terrorists.

The Jews learned terror from European, not Middle Eastern, pogroms and death camps. It is not surprising that they then use terror against the people who had what they wanted: a place free of terror. Palestine was an easy place for the West to steal because the people living there pre 1948 did not have modern weapons and they did not seem too eager to obtain them until the Balfour Declaration legitimized genocide against them.

Israel was not founded as a religious state. It was founded as a safe, secular haven for people who identified culturally as Jews. To many of them, if not most, their Jewishness was cultural more than religious. Of course, the state did take on a more religious tone later. But Israel is a product and perpetrator of terrorism in its inception and in its practices toward the people who inadvertently were in the way. I do not believe that the people of Israel considered their desperate struggle to survive by any means necessary, as fomenting terror. How many moral questions are resolved in the proverbial foxhole?

The Israelis do not have the means to change their political landscape. Not even the wall can save them. Tribes only last in isolation and the tribes of Israel are not isolated.

And think about terrorism in America. Do you think that African Americans are not aware that they have been terrorized? Do you think that we are unaware that the Ku Klux Klan, the White Citizens Councils, even elected authorities acted as terrorists?

BLP: *Is al-Qaa'ida, in your opinion, a terrorist organization?*

Supposing that what I've read and heard is true, yes, and I must reject it as an ugly abomination. I can find nothing in the Islamic tradition that would sanction such an ill-conceived agenda. It is numbingly non-Islamic. To base the destruction of the World Trade Center Twin Towers, for an example, on a fatwa making civilians legitimate targets makes me wonder how they harmonized their views with the tactics they desired.

I heard that Osama was angered that his offer to have his mujahideen protect the kingdom from the threat of Saddam Hussein was rejected in favor of the United States military. If this is true, imagine the affect of that blunder had they been delusional enough to agree to his plan. His soldiers would have literally become the state army of the kingdom by default and the wealth of the kingdom would have expanded his reach to every nation in the world with weapons ranging from OPEC nightmares to military interventions rivaling the Shi'a throughout the Arab and North African nations.

I'm not at all surprised that they emerged in Saudi Arabia. That is the land ruled by backward thinking. This is the home of intentional distortions, extreme tribalism, and intellectual decadence. The Arabs are given credit for amassing knowledge, expanding the sciences and contributing to the European Renaissance. The fact is, however, that those are Muslim achievements and not precisely Arab ones. The Arabs of today are a people damaged by colonialism and damned by oil.

If what I've learned about al-Qaa'ida is true, then it is in conflict with the message of the prophet who is purported to have said that we should seek knowledge wherever it is, the prophet who codified rules of war that spared women, children, trees, crops, and non-combatants.

So, I can't find any rationale, either in our Islamic tradition or my personal code of ethics that would rationalize al-Qaa'ida's barbarity.

BLP: *Do you believe in any form of revolution based on your understanding of Islam?*

Of course I do. But I do not credit Islam with my appreciation of the necessity to protect oneself by any means necessary. Even today, when an African American hears those words, "Any means necessary" the specter of al-Hajj Malik ash-Shabazz fills the spaces between them whether they are Muslim, Buddhist, Christian or Jewish because it speaks to a truth borne from suffering. It is human nature to want to survive and thrive.

Islam represented revolution to us. It does not, however, condone revolution except in extreme circumstances. There is an anecdote that explains this well. The prophet is purported to have said that we should change a bad situation with our hands. If we are prevented from doing this, then we should speak out against it. If we are prevented from doing this, then we should seek to change it in our hearts. The point being that we are, as Muslims, revolutionaries but not necessarily violent ones. Further, we will measure our tactics appropriate to the situation.

When I was younger, I was seduced by the romanticism of violent revolution. You remember the black berets of the Panther Party? Do you remember the H. Rap Brown question, "What will a penny buy?" (It bought a book of matches.) And, of course, "Burn baby burn!"

However, when I matured, I was able to see honestly how violent revolts led to other violent revolts and the end result was always a reign of terror and suffering of the people who were less able to protect themselves.

BLP: *Have you belonged to any Muslim organizations?*

Yes. I've belonged to more than a few. However, I first became interested in Islam as a result of listening to al-Hajji Malik Ash-Shabazz, then known as Malcolm X. His defiant, articulated strength was seductive to many of us. He made Islam politically relevant. I did have some knowledge of the Black Muslims as I grew up literally around the corner from Temple No. 1, which was in their cosmology Mecca, Chicago being Medina. You know the prophet started his mission in Mecca and completed it in Medina. So, Elijah Muhammad wanted to imitate that history. He didn't do much else in regard to imitating the prophet.

I wanted to join for political reasons but it was very clear that they weren't the real deal. All I had to do was read the Qur'an to eliminate them as a legitimate expression of Islam. In those days, the Black Muslims didn't want their followers to read the Qur'an unsupervised. But I couldn't accept that and I felt this was their attempt to control people's thoughts and beliefs.

BLP: *How did you get grounded in the knowledge of your faith?*

I took it on myself to read the Qur'an, cover to cover. This was difficult because there were many concepts, ideas, and perspectives new to me. I read footnotes, and checked references. Once having completed it, I turned my back on the Nation completely. I forgave Malcolm for following Elijah. Now, don't get me wrong. When Elijah and Malcolm taught that the white man was the devil, the evidence they presented was more than a little compelling.

Let me explain. They asked the African American people to judge people on how they behaved, both historically and contemporarily. At first, then, it was easy to conclude that most of the grievances I held against America were founded in the behavior of white people. So, the images of black men hanging from trees, tarred and feathered, Emmett Till's bloated corpse, the Klan, knowing how my parents and grandparents had been victims of America's racism, informed my political views. I did not understand until much later how racism had permitted me to behave in the same manner as white racists. I was permitted the privilege to group people by the quasi-scientific standards of race. It worked for me the same way it worked for them fundamentally. It is seductively facile to use race to explain behaviors. However, it is equally stupid.

Just prior to returning to Detroit from East Lansing, I had a profound spiritual experience that resulted in my knowing that I was Muslim. I just didn't have a notion of how to express it. Because of Malcolm, my first attempt to learn was to join the so-called Nation of Islam.

It was the discipline then for people seeking membership to copy verbatim a letter requesting to be considered for membership. I think I wrote a letter; I'm not certain. At any rate, I quickly became disenchanted with them. Maybe I made a few errors in the letter because I never got my X anyway.

For probably two years, I studied Islam alone. I tried to learn how to pray from illustrated books with hilarious results. I read everything I could get my hands on trying to fill my empty heart with the knowledge in these books. The more I read the more I realized that I had to find a way to express Islam socially. Islam was not, I discovered, a religion based on a personal relationship with the divine as its core principal; rather, Islam required social expression.

The problem was I didn't know any Muslims other than the pseudo-Muslims in the Nation.

I was married but didn't know how to engage my family in my new faith. My wife probably thought I had gone totally insane but she hung in there with me. I put her through a lot while I struggled to figure things out. I think I probably was insane. African Americans who think too much about their social and political reality are bound to go insane.

Finally, I found an old man named Hajj Samson. If I remember correctly, a mutual friend guided me to him. He was a legitimate Muslim. He had performed the hajj. He was a great help to me. He introduced me to the Arabic language and patiently guided me to perform the ritual prayer correctly. To be honest, he also had some unique ideas about Islam but they were harmless in comparison to the violence Elijah was doing to its core beliefs.

On Sundays I would bring the entire family to his mosque. I didn't ask them to pray with me; I really wanted them to grow comfortable with the idea of being with Muslims. For the most part, these meetings were quite enjoyable. He would always give a little talk and I appreciated much of what he had to say. However, some of what he said was very offensive to me.

He began to rant about how we could not have normal relationships with our grandparents because they were disbelievers. I loved my grandparents and my kids loved their grandparents and in every instance, they were good people. Yes, they were Christians but I understood that the Qur'an did not hold them in contempt and it was perfectly normal for a Muslim man to be married to a Christian woman. So, I questioned these teachings. He wouldn't relent so I felt I could no longer expose my children to him and that was that.

After returning to my college studies, I began to attend the Friday prayer in Dearborn Heights. There were mostly old men there. Many of them were from the Middle East although this was before the huge influx of Yemeni immigrants. I remember I used to give the imam rides after the prayer. He would always question me, "Do you have a job, my son?" I would reassure him but he would eventually ask me again. You see I was working a shift that allowed me to attend the prayer. That was pretty unusual. There were only a few African Americans attending that mosque at the time.

Later, I became involved with a group of younger, wild-eyed African American men. By this time, my Arabic was pretty good. These guys knew less than me about the ritual prayers and Islam in general. Someone once described them as having the vibrations of Bedouin warriors. How romantic is that? Actually, their madness had an energy that I had never witnessed. But along with that energy was a profound desperation that discolored their efforts so that I could never fully invest in wherever they were headed.

Later, after finishing my BA at a local university I was awarded a fellowship to study Arabic. By that time, I was very involved in the local African American Muslim community.

I also joined the Muslim Students Association. I worked for a short time with the Islamic Teaching Center. I also joined the Muslim Brotherhood.

BLP: *You are a member of the Muslim Brotherhood?*

Were. Many years ago, a very good friend made it possible. But I was not emotionally equipped to manage such a commitment. I was also facing the dilemma of knowing the direction our rhetoric was pointing us and being uncomfortable with the assumptions and goals implicit in it.

Finally, I realized that I did not share, as a personal goal, participating in proselytizing and that essentially is what the Ikhwaan (Muslim Brothers) must do in the U.S.

BLP: *Who was the first person you ever loved?*

I was told the subject of the interview was my life as a Muslim intellectual and activist. What does this question have to do with any of that?

BLP: *I thought that I might get to know more about you as a human being.*

I wonder what your response would have been had I said something other than my mother or my first caregiver if she or he had been someone other than my mother. Am I being defensive? Probably. But you have to understand that being who I am, I have the right to be defensive.

Your question assumes a lot.

BLP: *What do you mean?*

I mean your question assumes that we're operating with the same lexicon just because we share a language. But, you know, we actually may have, and probably do have, quite distinct glosses. I grew up in a segregated town. We, the minority of record, prided ourselves on our language being impenetrable to outsiders.

Even when our phrases were borrowed, we'd either drop them or alter their meanings. It is a misconception that we wanted to be like the majority; we loved differences that defined us. What we didn't like was how we were denied even treatment. By definition, we were unequal among equals. The stain of servility was inappropriately seen as something more than a consequence of being terrorized, captured, transported, and being forced to labor.

The burying grounds are crowded with those of us who refused the stain. This is the history from which I've come.

Back to your question: my answer might not be at all what you expect or want to hear.

BLP: *I'm willing to be surprised.*

My first love, as yours, was the creator. This love was expressed long before I was a human being.

BLP: *Please explain.*

Take a walk with me. There was a trans-historical moment, where the creator had us recognize the creator – created relationship as one of profound love. We Muslims believe that in that moment the creator asked us, asked our souls, "Am I not your creator and sustainer?" And we said, "Yes." This, then, was our first moment of consciousness; this was our first moment as Muslims – all of us.

Thus, when I was born I had already experienced such a deep love that I was born experienced in the ways of love of such a dimension that all other loves are pale imitations in comparison.

Can you get to that?

Then the birthing process, the clothing of my soul if you will, made me forgetful of that primordial covenant. In that forgetfulness, the intimacy of the mother – child relationship may have confused this soul. In other words, the love I have for my mother and father may have seemed preeminent but only because of the forgetfulness that I was to overcome through my pursuit of the truth Islam promised to provide.

BLP: *I must admit that you surprised me. Is this a standard view in Islam?*

Actually, all Muslims believe this because it is explicit in the Qur'an. I won't bore you with citations. Look it up. But remember that this covenant applies to all of us. It is not based on religious preferences.

BLP: *From this, then, is it fair for me to say that all Muslims believe that their first love was Allah?*

I don't mean to insult you but how else could it be? Given that we necessarily believe in the Qur'an?

BLP: *How do you feel about our capacity to love another human being? One could construe your comment as an indictment of that concept.*

Listen man, every chapter of the Qur'an begins with an expression that indirectly honors our mothers. The creator describes in that expression the creator – created relationship as mother to child. So when you understand that, you understand why my love for my mother is authentic and why my love of the creator is so complete that it cannot really be described in earthly terms.

Every chapter with the exception of the ninth begins with the basmala. This expression is translated as in the name of Allah, the compassionate, the merciful. The Arabic words for compassion and merciful are derived from the word for womb.

BLP: *Where were you born?*

I was born in Detroit, Michigan. I was born in a black owned an operated hospital. I left my mother's womb for the hands of a black physician. Black nurses cared for me. My birth was a totally black experience. Of course, I was told most of this but some of it I just figured out on my own.

What difference does it make where I was born? I think you may want to locate me somewhere so you can justify your biases. When I tell people that I was born in Detroit, some might suspect that I was born in the ghetto with junkies, gangs, prostitutes and other marginalized people vying for my soul. In reality I was born into a very solid community. This thriving community had a strong working class orientation but there were also doctors, lawyers, teachers, and house painters, the chronically unemployed and under-employed persons.

A single mother did not raise me. I had a father, siblings, and a bunch of relatives living nearby. Our neighbors were also an extension of our family. It was popular a few years ago to say what some purport to be an African adage: it takes a village to raise a child. Well, an extended family with supportive neighbors raised my siblings and me. I don't want you to go away thinking otherwise.

BLP: *What other prejudices do you think people have about people born in Detroit?*

If we're talking about white people born in Detroit, the assumptions would be mostly benign. If you're talking about African Americans, then the assumptions would center on violence, drugs, blight, and hopelessness. And don't forget the music. Where would America be without Motown? You guys would still be singing about how much that doggy in the window cost; you know, the one with the wagging tail.

But Motown music came from the suffering behind the stereotypes. It wasn't nothing but the blues dressed up. But white people got sick with it. You know what I mean? Eventually white people wanted to dress like us, walk like us, and even sing like us; but that's alright because you can never be what you ain't.

BLP: *Was music important to you growing up?*

It certainly was. My mother played the piano as did her siblings. They also sang. Most of their playing and singing centered on the church. My father's family was also musical. My grandfather was an accomplished musician and one of my uncles was a professional musician.

There were many other musical influences. Detroit, being a favorite northern city for those escaping the brutality of the south, became a home to the Blues. There was also the solid musical education available in the public schools and spurred by an innate entrepreneurial spirit, saw the creation of recording companies that flourished as small businesses in the African American community. Motown was the most successful. Gordy's genius was recognizing that the Blues required a format that could accompany the rise of an African American urban middle class or at least our aspirations to become middle class.

Then, in the late 50s and early 60s, jazz exploded in my head and musicians like John Coltrane, Miles Davis, Cannonball Adderley, Charlie Parker, Nina Simone... the list goes on — encouraged me and influenced me politically. I also should mention Ahmad Jamal because he tied it all together from the Muslim point of view. He combined music with the ethic of Islam. He wasn't really a religious influence on me but the idea of Islam being compatible with music was certainly noted.

There were essentially two very public men who influenced my politico-spiritual development: John Coltrane and al-Hajj Malik ash-Shabazz.

And music remains important to me. My perspective has certainly broadened but the music that I loved then I still love. Actually, I now prefer the unvarnished Blues. As kids we would sometimes stand outside of bars and listen to players like John Lee Hooker and Washboard Willie.

BLP: *What is your fondest memory of your parents from your childhood?*

My parents gave us a lot of good memories. Not a single memory stands above the rest. I just remember a real fullness of life. We never wanted for anything. We were well fed, clothed, educated, and most of all loved. They gave us that old fashion love you know what I mean? That love that sometimes wore your behind out if you did something wrong, especially something that embarrassed the family. That was preeminent: do not embarrass your family.

BLP: *Did they follow a religious tradition? If so, which one(s)?*

My parents were Christians. My mother was raised in the Baptist church but I don't think my father's parents were that much into a specific religion. I got the notion that they were what I would call Christians by default.

Later, while my father was away in the army, she converted to Catholicism. I guess my father followed her when he returned from the service. They raised us as Catholics. They even sent us to Catholic school. It is surprising how many Muslims I know who went to Catholic school.

She eventually abandoned Catholicism and returned to her roots in the Baptist tradition, even the same church. I never asked her why. But, to me, the Catholics were pretty weird.

I remember once, when I was first enrolled in Catholic school a nun became very angry with me because I was sitting at my desk with my hands in my lap. She thought I was masturbating! How crazy is that? I'm sitting in class, trying to pay attention to whatever it was she was teaching and she freaks because my hands were in my lap. Don't misunderstand me. I knew about masturbation and I was probably masturbating by then. But in school? Please. Even now I consider all aspects of my sex life to be private. I wouldn't have wanted anyone in that class to know that I masturbated.

All of my classmates, except for a few of the boys, seemed to be lobotomized. They were obedient little automatons. I can still hear those, "Yes, Sister; no Sister, may I Sister". They made those kids little sniffling sycophants.

But there is where I think I first became intellectually aware of Muslims. I do remember something about the Crusades. Not that I would have made any religious connection at that time, I mean I was only 9 years old or so. I think I was drawn to them the same way I was drawn to the Confederate army. They were, in my mind, the underdogs. They were rebellious and I was certainly feeling like an underdog then. For some reason, I had a lot of rebellion in me in those days. I sensed without knowing that my world was not right.

But there were things about Catholicism that I really liked. There were things about the Baptist tradition that I liked, too. The mass was very seductive. The priest all dressed up, mumbling incoherently as he performed sacred magic and then fed us its results. How cool was that? Man, I had to get a part of that magic so

I became an altar boy. I learned to mumble incoherently. I learned to pour the water and the wine. I learned to carry the paten just below the chin of the communicant to catch any Jesus crumbs that might not make it from the priest's hand to the communicant's mouth.

I even considered becoming a priest. I told my mother and she patiently began saving pennies so that I might attend the seminary one day. When I finally realized that to be a priest I had to take a vow of celibacy, I gave that dream up. I had not yet had sex but the idea of never doing what I so anxiously looked forward to just didn't work for me.

Altar boys were the coolest dudes because they were in on the magic. We helped the priest robe up. We even got a chance to drink a little of the wine because we were always there before the priest. I don't remember it tasting very good. Sometimes, when we would pour the wine into the priest's chalice, he would signal us to keep it flowing. I thought, even then, that this dude likes his wine.

I think they reinforced an idea I had about god being very remote and historical. None of the good stuff seemed to have happened recently. It's like since he gave some white people a chance a long time ago, we could forget about good stuff happening in our time. Of course I thought god was white taking care of white people because they were the best people. It all seems stupid now but that's the way it was.

BLP: *Do you remember what they taught you about the Crusades?*

No, not really. I just remember that there were pictures in a book that showed Muslims riding horses probably with their swords drawn as the good guys defeated them for god's sake. The crusaders took the Holy Land back from the barbaric hordes. Some of these ideas are probably false memories. You know, I probably learned some of this stuff later but it was such a connection even then that I do recall something very romantic happened.

BLP: *Did you encounter other instances where Islam played a role?*

Actually, I did. I had an uncle who had been a merchant marine. During his travels, he had come in contact with Muslims. I'm not certain just where in the world he encountered them but he did have a copy of a Qur'an. I was amazed at the beauty of the letters on the page as well as the flowery margins. I do not know whether he was a Muslim; I don't think he ever told me one way or another.

Even at this early age, I knew that I was headed for something other than the usual fare of Christianity. I was a rebel.

BLP: *When did you become a Muslim?*

It was January 1966. It was a typical Michigan January: cold and snow covered. I knew at a certain moment that I was a Muslim. There was no one there to welcome me or to teach me what it meant to be a Muslim on a day-to-day basis. So I just began to read more and more and to introduce myself as a Muslim. There was no more alcohol, no more pork in my life. Odd as it seems today, I still smoked marijuana.

So I embraced the one true faith in the dead of winter staring out from two glass patio doors at a frozen creek with ice-burdened trees bending over it. I think it fair to say that my family and friends understood my conversion for what it was at the core: a political statement. Although it had a definite spiritual background, Malcolm X was in the foreground and my newly adopted faith system gave definition to everything social.

BLP: *After Hajj Samson, who was your most influential teacher?*

There were not many teachers of Islam available to me in the earliest days. There were older, more experienced Muslims around Detroit but most of them were so politically conservative that I avoided them from the perspective of learning about Islam. There were the old men in Dearborn who taught me the power of proselytizing by being consistent in one's behavior. In other words, if you just behave as a Muslim should in every circumstance, someone, probably someone searching, would ask you about something you'd done giving you the opportunity to mention something about Islam without seeming to recruit them.

This stood in stark contrast to the traveling groups brothers that called themselves Tabliq jama'a from places like Pakistan who actually taught against any kind of political action and presented themselves in such an odd fashion that they put off all who weren't already attuned to their way of thinking.

I certainly had no practical use for them. As far as the local brothers were concerned, too many eschewed work but enjoyed the pleasures of polygyny. These brothers had the temerity to suggest that by my working and supporting my family I was actually supporting the devil's handiwork. They pled with me to join them in their idleness. But there was no way I could divorce my roots as a working class youth stretching my hand into the middle class.

Where was I to find a teacher? So, I settled for someone to teach me Arabic. As I worked to complete my undergraduate degree, I began the formal study of Arabic. I was fortunate in that I found a teacher with passion for the language and an acceptance of me as an African American Muslim in need of that language. We worked well together. I learned a great deal from her.

She prepared me for the next big step. She and my wife encouraged me to apply for a fellowship to study Arabic. I won the fellowship and was accepted to graduate school.

Graduate school was challenging in the best manner. The faculty was supportive in every way except my being a Muslim. The only Muslims in the department were intimidated by the times and cowed by their fear of being ostracized if they became known as Muslim activists. The instruction and guidance was excellent. I was encouraged, coached, cajoled and ridiculed for my benefit.

Fortunately, I did become active with the Muslim Students Association. Although there still was no teacher to be found, I learned a great deal from interacting with these students and their families.

Three or four years later, I won a fellowship to study with an eminent Muslim scholar who was my first real teacher. He introduced me to the disciplined study of Islamic law and hadith literature. It was through his profound imagination that I gained comfort with the mythic elements of the Qur'an. He forced me to confront the humanity that is buried within those myths and how to use those dynamic aspects to grasp the fundamental dimension of Islam.

Isma'il Raji al-Farouqi led me through the dense forest of Islamic traditions, cutting a path for me through its under-story and helped me soar above its canopy. He taught the practical importance of forgiveness.

He led me to work with the Nation of Islam as it struggled to find a more dynamic program of inclusion and expansion. Those in Philadelphia were still debilitated by their criminal backgrounds and their distrust of people and ideas from literally another world.

With his encouragement, I studied more than Islamic law. I searched the literature on Muslims in America and formed a few well-developed theories that other scholars were later to justify. I theorized without much evidence although there was a spattering of incidents, that a syncretic form of Islam was brought to the Americas in the hearts of some of those captured and shipped here. That these concepts, already with a distinct, syncretic West African expression, were the basis for some of the maroon societies as well as African – Native peoples connections.

The mass of these ideas was dense enough to survive slavery and to find later expression in movements such as the Moorish Scientists and the Nation of Islam. Certainly the movement these survivals created later informed Muslim immigrants.

The more I lived within this milieu, the more discontented I became because the humanity was so stultifying. There seemed to be little difference between the mundane life of a Muslim and the mundane life of a Christian. I was becoming so disenchanted that I began to loose interest in the principles that men and women have died to defend and propagate. I was forced to admit that my faith may have had a less than noble beginning as it was found on the racial turmoil within the Western empire and little else. I was forced to engage actual Muslims and not the heroes I wanted. Thus, my crisis of faith had more dimensions than I had words to describe them.

BLP: *You have been to many Islamic countries, one of them being the Sudan. What do you think of Shaykh H.?*

First, before I speak of the Shaykh, let me say that there are really no Islamic countries although several have included Islam in their names, in their founding and legitimizing documents. To declare a country Islamic is very controversial in Islamic political thought. The concept of an Islamic nation is bastardization, to some, of the concept of Ummah. The concept of nation is an outgrowth of tribalism. It is convenient shorthand that is actually contrary to the political structure alluded to in the Qur'an and the clarifying example of the prophet and his immediate successors even beyond Islam's sectarian developments.

But there is really no blueprint for governance in the Qur'an. There are, nevertheless, principles of social organization, explicit and implicit, in the Qur'an that should serve as the basis for the development of political structures. Frankly, I wouldn't consider any religious doctrine as politically definitive. Regardless of whatever safeguards we could construct, there would always be some social statuses preferred over others.

There are Muslim thinkers who believe Islam is compatible with nationalism but I see it very differently. Nations compete so ferociously that eventually they kill one another. This philosophical extension of tribalism is not compatible with Islamic values and those apologists have it wrong.

As ironic as it seems given today's turmoil, Muslims can only thrive in political democracies.

I first met the Shaykh while he was visiting the United States. He spoke at an MSA convention. He was ready made for us in several ways. He gave us a refreshing look at Islamic law. For example, according to jurists, if a married woman accepts Islam and her husband does not, she must divorce him. Well, the Shaykh theorized that, based on early practice codified as the Maliki School, that this was not the first option. That worked for us. We were struggling to create families and to break up families on any bases was obviously counterproductive.

I again met the Shaykh in the Sudan. I had been invited there to give a speech at a Khartoum University student organized function. At that time, my Arabic was pretty good. As a matter of fact, although the Sudanese were fluent in English, they told me they understood my Arabic better than my English. I thought this was hilarious. Anyway, I gave my talk for a second time, in Arabic by the Nile River, under a stand of trees that the students called a forest.

When my speech was over, one of the students approached me and asked how long I had been a member of the Muslim Brotherhood. I explained that I wasn't and he smiled and said that of course I was. His evidence was how I gave my talk in their manner, how the people who had arranged my visit were members, and how everyone who had attended what they called the First Cultural Season importantly noticed this.

It finally dawned on me who I was working with and for. I attended a meeting at the home of the Shaykh. We all sat in a big circle and introduced ourselves to one another. I met Muslims that night that had been incarcerated because of their beliefs. I felt a strong bond with them.

We wanted to join the brotherhood but there was a huge political struggle that we had no real role in. They would not allow us totally in. I guess we weren't really trusted. They probably recognized us for who we were. We were full of zeal but we had never really been tested in any serious way. We were an unknown quantity. On the other hand we certainly didn't want to hook up with the Muslims from Pakistan. These brothers did not have half a chance of being successful here because of cultural and racial identity issues. These brothers did not like music. They had no swagger.

But the brothers from the Sudan were infused with that negritude vibe and we wanted to roll with them. The leadership (probably the Shaykh) did not want us in the organization. Nevertheless, at least one of the brothers trusted us enough to invite us into the brotherhood.

During those days, there was hardly any consideration of Muslims as terrorists or anti-Western. Of course, the undercurrents of those times nourished the armed movements so many fear today.

We did not view the brothers from Africa as violent. Of course, we were aware of their armed struggle in the Sudan. Naturally and naively in retrospect, we automatically sided with our friends. I am not suggesting that they were the lesser of our choices but I am rueful of not examining other positions.

We believed that if we behaved to the higher personal standards of our religion rather than create and enforce norms on others; recruited carefully selected young people to build a strong core leadership group; engaged our communities in social and political discussions; and did these consistently and patiently that Islam would take its roots here – or should I say re-root itself – in this land and in the right way.

It is true that Islam addresses war as a terrible but creative process. It should be the last resort to the defense of Muslims and the weak. There is no offensive role for Muslim armies in the world. The Muslim's duty to his faith is to spread it but not through violent or aggressive means. There is no compulsion in these matters.

If these principles seem naïve, then we were but we never supported the kinds of acts that we see today. Some of the people that are now described as terrorists were our teachers and this violence is not what we were taught.

Perhaps they realized that our expression of Islam was contextualized by the religious moderation exhibited in our nation. Extremism seems to melt away under public scrutiny. I could no more imagine American Muslims engaged in subversive activities than I could imagine Catholics rampaging on orders from the pope.

Of course, there is always that alienated romantic ready to sacrifice his life for a soon to be forgotten headline.

When confronted with the logic of the lesser jihad, which is to say, military rather than spiritual struggle, most American Muslims would acknowledge the great unlikelihood of this happening here.

BLP: *Even if the rhetoric increases and violence against Muslims becomes routine, do you visualize losing your reluctance to engage in jihad?*

The question that you seem to be asking is whether I would engage in armed struggle against my country under any circumstances. This makes me feel like I've been wasting time attempting to get you to understand that jihad is not at all what you want it to be. If anyone were attacked, I would recommend self-defense.

In the Arabic language, the phrase, "reluctant jihadist" would be "al-mujaahid al-muqawaama" which really suggests someone on the brink of acting, not someone refusing to act. Remember what I said: I can envision situations, defensive to be sure, in which Muslims take up arms.

BLP: *Thank you for consenting to this interview and sharing your views with us.*

SMOKE FROM THE MACHINE

1. Wednesday, February 4, 2004

HALLIBURTON TO REPAY GOV'T $27M FOR OVERCHARGES

ANOTHER BURDEN?
Islam has been very, very good to me. The connective practice of prayer calms my heart and unites me with a vibrant and complex community. The fasting slows being in the world so I may take the time to look inward and see the real work (jihad) to be done. Performing the pilgrimage to Mecca caused my examination of the historical and social dimensions of my faith. Dropping money into the lives of those who have less without the embarrassment of proximity and identity purifies the money I keep.

Wasn't it enough of a burden that I was born African American? What drove me to embrace a religion virtually unknown yet feared by my fellow Americans? At the outset, it had a great deal to do with the proselytizing of al-Hajj Malik ash-Shabazz (AKA Malcolm X). Like many American Muslims, I expected a community of Muslims to emerge from the remains of the Nation of Islam and the ethnically diverse communities of Muslims from the east coast to Hawaii. I thought he represented the onset of a golden age of religious and political awareness.

After beginning the study of Arabic, followed by history and culture, Muslim traditions, and Islamic law, I traveled to the Middle East and Africa to see what I could of how Islam was practiced contemporarily. Of course, I found as much diversity as the world could imagine. I've lived and prayed with Muslims from Albania, Saudi Arabia, Philadelphia, Kano, England, Malaysia, China, Nigeria, and Canada. What I did learn was that Islam has as many expressions as there are cultures and as many permeations as subcultures within each.

The simplicity of Islam is its elegance. The superficial simplicity of monotheism is seductive but like all trysts, the entanglements are profound and, if understood, life altering. There are no notions of minor gods, a trinity of gods, or any other thing that some may desire to worship. However, everywhere I turned I saw the shadows of precursor faiths or belief systems. The elegance, then, is transformed into a kaleidoscope of textures, behaviors, and attitudes emanating from the same thing.

The impact of these variations should not be minimized. The classic sectarian struggle between the Sunni and the Shi'a is one of many fractious moments in the life history of the Muslim world. To assume these differences will be put aside to achieve the greater purpose of world domination or at least the ushering out of the Western world's hegemony is to engage in pulp fiction.

The Islam Muslims in America embrace is a pared down version with some discoloring substrata from the various cultures that served as hosts and transmitters. These discolorations of Islam's fabric appeared regionally mirroring the new homes of the immigrants.

It is on us to inform this pared down Islam with our own cultural traditions. To the extent that our Americanism is confluent with Islam, we don't have to speculate different ways of being. Yet we reflect the various cultures that are expressed even within the oldest American ethnic groups. African Americans bring their traditions, mores, and customs, as do European Americans. These various expressions will come together unequally to forge a generalized identity that doesn't succeed in describing any single group adequately.

This means, in effect, that the fractious nature of American society will be reflected in the stratifications of Islam. The profound racial crevasse that traverses the imagination of the nation will be reflected in Muslim America.

I speculate that some of my ancestors were Muslims. This is more likely given that I am a descendant of the Seminole Maroons of Fort Clark, Brackettville, Texas. The explicit goal of the tribe was to settle in a land of peace where they could raise crops and herds to feed their families. They did not care whether they stayed at the fort, or relocated to Indian Territory or Africa.

Not unlike the jihadists soldiering in the Fulani Jihads, the Mascogos, as they were known in Mexico (which also recognized them as a free people), wanted to settle after they had practiced the art of war successfully for so many years. Everywhere they had gone, they had soldiered. They led the Seminoles to successful campaigns in Florida, aiding greatly that tribe's survivability.

The Seminoles did not understand the Mascogos desire to retire from war and to live simply, raising crops and tending their animals. This was a source of conflict that was exacerbated by the political shifts in the leadership of the Seminole nation that began to reflect confederate racism. This accented the differences in goals they had expressed as long ago as Florida.

2. Thursday, February 5, 2004

SAUDIS ACCOUNT FOR 1/4 OF GITMO DETAINEES

WHOSE WAR IS IT, ANYWAY?
George Tenet now says that there was no imminent threat to the US from Iraqi weapons of mass destruction (WMD). I think Bush wanted Tenet to be the good soldier, like Colin Powell, and take a bullet for him but Tenet thought about it and said, "Nope. Whose war was it? It wasn't mine!"

This war against terrorism is really an attack on language, its verbicide. One cannot war against a tactic. Muslims feel at risk because this limited police action is taking place in their world. They know that there are bombs smart enough to find each of their homes on any crowded street or their shack in any crowded refugee camp.

To strengthen his case, Bush has chosen a new strategy: we're "making democracy work" in the Middle East. This sounds like a workable plan. Invade a nation, destroying its infrastructure, jail its leaders, fuel the insurgency by disbanding the military, and then instruct them on the choices they have for their democratic government. Other forms, such as dictatorship, theocracy, hereditary rule, anarchy, were not even on the table which means they couldn't vote for them. Is this democracy at work?

Which form of democracy does he feel is more appropriate: direct democracy, proportional democracy or representative democracy? Should the Iraqis be able to elect their leadership directly or do they need an electoral college? Think about it: Gore got more popular votes than Bush but Bush had the electoral college and the supreme court on his side. Is this the type of democracy for Iraq?

Even apparently simple answers from Bush forces us to admit his limitations, intellectual but more importantly, ethical.

3. Tuesday, February 10, 2004

ANTI-US ATTACKS RAGE ON IN IRAQ AS SHI'ITE MUSLIMS PLEAD FOR ELECTIONS

DISSEMBLING BUSH
The Republican Party seems to own the American dictionary and, therefore, the political debate in the United States. Their mavens have defined their economic program as "Tax Relief". Since we only seek relief from bad things, as more than one commentator has pointed out, then the tenor of the debate is basically set by that one phrase.

The Democrats are known as the party of "Tax and Spend" which suggests that the money will be used unwisely. Bush, to mimic an expression made famous by Bush the Elder, says, "Read my lips: no new taxes... but plenty of new spending!" He is, I suppose, demonstrating his version of compassionate conservatism in the costliest of fashions.

Talk about an irresponsible electorate. Clinton lied about oral sex and we suffered through an impeachment hearing while Bush lied about WMD (costing the lives of over 500 Americans – injuring thousands while killing thousands of Iraqis). There is no call for impeachment hearings.

Behind the masks of liberation and democratization are faces: big, soft, and piggish at the trough gulping America's future and that of the Iraqis – eating both nations out of house and home. These corporations have no national allegiances. The only thing they want from us is that we remain voracious consumers. It is not important whether you vote; the majority of voters chose Gore but the US Supreme Court chose Bush. Is this the kind of democracy the US is granting to Iraq?

Perhaps a proportional system? It is not good enough for Americans but its good enough for Iraqis. The Shi'a will get 60 percent of the power, the Sunni will get 30 percent; the Kurds will get 8 percent and the rest of the minorities will get what's left. Why can't we have the same system here? Do you think that Latinos and African Americans (the ones who are not Latino) trust the government to ensure that they get their fair shares of the wealth and power?

I don't think so, either.

4. Tuesday, February 17, 2004

CATHOLIC CHURCH: 11,000 CHILDREN ABUSED BY PRIESTS OVER PAST 50 YEARS

AN HONEST MUSLIM
As the wars in the Muslim world rage on, it is important for us, the direct and indirect victims of these wars, to face some fundamental facts about the wars' origins. Probably none of us remember the "War to end all wars" also popularly known as WW I.

The last remnant of the Muslim Empire was destroyed along with the Turkish government, by that time a very weak caliphate, and fell into the hands of the European powers. Since that time Muslims in the so-called Middle East have longed for the day when they would exact their revenge on Western Europe.

Muslims are required to be under Islamic political authority if they are to be in full accord with the Qur'an. This is the dark secret that Muslims don't want to talk about.

The Shi'a have a history of giving deference to their Imams. The Sunnis, as ironic as it is, present a more democratic approach that has resulted in a dispersal of authority. Organizations such as the Muslim Brotherhood may have formed in response to that apparent void. The Brotherhood's disciplines do reveal its genesis is associated with Sufi brotherhoods. The founding members used those disciplines as well as a political consciousness rationalized in the revival of the caliphate.

The Muslim Brotherhood has spawned a plethora of organizations the most publicized being the Palestinian Hamas. Some of these organizations imitate Shi'a organizational tactics such as suicide bombings. As an umbrella organization, the Brothers lose their credibility, at least on my street, because I cannot rationalize killing in any other context than defensive. Most of the Western world customarily engages in debate without the interference of the state. If Muslims in America want to make the best case for Islam they can do it without harming anyone.

America, under Bush the Second, has exacerbated the problem. He has driven Americans, Muslims and others, to the precipice of a hellish end.

So, an honest Muslim faces this conundrum. We need a way out. Dethrone Bush the Second. Dethrone the Iranian Mullahs. Dethrone Osama and the other terrorists. And let us then suffer peacefully as we muddle our way through to the realization of our political dreams.

Is there, then, any real distinction between honest Muslims and just honest people? Not a drop. So you be honest, too.

5. Friday, February 20, 2004

SAN FRANCISCO SUES CALIFORNIA OVER GAY MARRIAGE

A LEAGUE OF THEIR OWN
The Bush League (once known as the US government) has invaded two Muslim nations and threatens a third. Those sensitive Muslims among us look at this as a war against Islam. Sometimes, I feel the same way. But rationality forces me to ask: Why? Is the Bush League attempting to foist Christianity on the entire world? I don't think so, at least when I'm being rational.

Rather, the BL is attempting to lessen the cost of extracting the natural resources of the region. We need it. They got it. Simple: supply and demand.

With the most powerful nation in the world gathering her forces in the Middle East, the nations there are mired in confusion and self-defeating policies and actions.

When Saddam changed the mode of exchange for Iraqi oil from the dollar to the euro, he threatened the US's stranglehold on the world economy. Since the takeover of Iraq, the BL changed the mode of exchange back to the dollar. Now we can all rest peacefully in the knowledge that the dollar is a bit more secure (unless you're a grunt driving a Hummer through Baghdad).

Iran is losing its soul to a bunch of clerics who want to make certain that everyone is properly dressed, making their 5 daily prayers, avoiding all of the unseemliness of the modern world while the US marshals its forces waiting for the opportunity to topple the ayatollahs. Because beneath the appearance of bumbling is the reality of a government extending its influence into every nook and cranny of the Middle East. Iran has designs on the region that amount to the establishment of a regionally defined Islamic government as the basis for the resurgent caliphate.

Saudi Arabia, the richest corporate government in the world, is spinning with discontent. How long before the BL offers to support that totalitarian regime with troops? You see, democracy is good for Iraq but not for Saudi Arabia. It is difficult to feel any sympathy for these corrupt governments although I feel it is horrific for the BL to drag us through the sand to topple them. Let their own people take care of their problems. Pay for the oil and drive away.

If Muslim nations can't handle their business, there'll always be someone waiting to help out, even if they're not invited. This is a cold world and it is unforgiving to those who idle away their time and resources on vanities whether they be politico-religious or socio-political.

Pray for peace. Pray for sanity. Pray that BL gets bumped to the sidelines by a reasonable... Okay, okay. Let's hope that when the BL is retired by election, that whatever we get is at least a little better. Incremental justice? This might be a new concept brewing!

6. Wednesday, March 3, 2004

WORLDCOM CEO BERNARD EBBERS INDICTED

PROGRESSIVE ISLAM?
Lately, I have read and heard people discussing the concept of progressive Islam. This is a paradigm-defining concept. Progressive Islam requires that there be a narrow-minded Islam or a regressive Islam.

Progressive Islam suggests restating Islamic beliefs and adjusting its practice in a manner more accessible to Western sensibilities. Its not Islam that can be categorized as progressive, narrow, or regressive; rather, it is Muslims who have these characteristics. However, the marketing of Islam to the West requires that Muslims put on their best cloak, adopt a modern ethos, and embrace another nation's perverted obsession with Jeffersonian democracy.

Muslims retained pre-Islamic customs and adopted customs of other cultures from the beginning of Islam's preaching. This is, in and of itself, not problematic. It is also not progressive. It is the rule, not the exception, that the community informs the context in which faith is practiced.

This principle has been enshrined, if you will, in Islamic jurisprudence. During the time that the Muslim Community was led by Umar ibn al-Khattab, Muslim armies found a community in North Africa where the people held farmlands in common. There was no private ownership of land. Islamic law supports the private ownership of property and presents within the Qur'an inheritance guidelines that were precise enough to generate a mathematical science we know today as algebra.

The jurists recognized that this process of distributing property rights was not workable in this environment. The people were encouraged to retain their practices although those practices were contrary to the text of the Qur'an. Everyone was satisfied because Islamic law was adapted to the needs of the people.

Perhaps the progressives want to go farther than this example implies. For example, I know of a "progressive" Islamic center that has successfully opened a community school. The children are taught to pledge allegiance to the flag of the United States of America. The pledge they are taught does have a prologue that honors Islam but pledging allegiance to a flag seems tantamount to idol worship. A Muslim's allegiance is first to Allah. Citizenship does not require that we pledge allegiance to the flag. It is appropriate that we acknowledge the government's authority and our loyalty to the nation.

Muslims may align themselves with community leaders but never to a symbol. If I were to meet a person dedicated to Islamic principles and willing to organize Muslims to pursue the goals of Islam, I could see pledging my allegiance to him. What does it mean to be allegiant to a flag after all? The implication for me is that the one who does is actually pledging allegiance to the government's chief executive officer. In this case, which is the American case, that's a lying dissembling ex-cocaine head with bloody hands.

I hope that this modernization is not a code word for Westernization. Don't get me wrong. I think that Muslims should adopt their practice of Islam to the real circumstances of their lives. For example, there are some Muslims who actually believe that listening to music is forbidden. Well, I love listening to music and it doesn't have to qualify as religious. As a matter of fact, I listen to the blues quite often (Son House, Taj Mahal, Muddy Waters, Mississippi John Hurt, etc.) I listen to jazz (John Coltrane, Keith Jarrett, etc.)

The Muslims residing in the West will not be the source of the reawakening of the Muslim world because no one will know what they are talking about. No one in the so-called Muslim world will be able to relate to the specific issues that we face in the West. They, instead, are focused on more basic issues that we have lost sight of because we are so rich we do not consider what it might be like to be a subsistence farmer in a land besieged by a spreading desert and under the thumb of rapacious Western societies.

7.   Monday, March 8, 2004

ARISTIDE TELLS REPORTERS: I WAS KIDNAPPED BY U.S.

SCUFFLING FOR RECOGNITION
The more I learn about my ancestors, the more I want to learn. I am related to the Warriors some of whom are called Ward. This gives me a sense of belonging to an international tradition of struggle for social justice.

I'm related to other folks whose names I do not know and the impenetrable emptiness around those roots leaves me coldly ignorant about who they were and how they lived.

This is my rant for today: recognize First Nations people; honor the treaties. I don't know what's gotten into us, needing your recognition I mean. I know that I've been here; worked here, long enough to say this is my home no matter how you feel about it. You may have to remind yourself periodically that I have the right, not the privilege, to vote but I know that I am a citizen and an honorable person.

8.   Wednesday, March 10, 2004

RARE HURRICANE FORMS IN SOUTH ATLANTIC

WHAT'S IN A NAME?
I became a Muslim in 1966. I changed my name in 1968. This was no small event as it heralded possible alienation from my family and all the histories, nuances of being and future connectivity associated with it. I didn't announce it right away because I wanted them to see that I had not changed fundamentally, that I was not rejecting them, and that, above all else, except God, I loved them. They would then understand that this change in faith and name as an embracing of a very personal truth.

My mother and my grandmother rode the train from Detroit to San Antonio to see my great grandmother when my mother was pregnant. My great grandmother, Elsie Ward Taylor, named me. The name she gave me is associated with the historic figure, Tony Warrior, her grandfather.

It may be that some of the Mascogos were Muslims or descended from Muslims. The behaviors cited in historic documents suggest a connection. Additionally, from the writings of Kenneth Wiggins Porter, we know that there was at least one Arab traveling with John Horse and Tony Warrior when they first entered Mexico.

I am proudly a descendant of Africans, Mascogos, Muslims, Christians, Animists, Europeans, Mexicans – all of this tumbled together. Look at your names to learn what you can so that you might stand somewhere comfortably aware.

9. Monday, March 15, 2004

U.S. CONSIDER MILITARY DRAFT FOR SPECIALISTS

WAKE UP CITIZENS OF THE CONSUMER EMPIRE!
The quagmire in Iraq poses several problems for us as citizens of the empire. The quagmire was created, in fact, because there is an empire whose shadow stretches even beyond the grasp of the sun. Every lesser nation (all nations are lesser) is on bended knee waiting for the blessing or the curse from the titular head of the empire, Bush the Second.

We live in the luxury we demand from the Consumer Empire. Yet we complain about the means used to maintain this luxury. What would happen if the Consumer Empire were to retract its bloody claws from the throats of lesser nations? Would we be content to live with gasoline costing 7 or 8 dollars a gallon? If bananas were $2.50 each? If your rent were $12,500 a month? How liberal would you be then?

Even the victims of this greed and the descendants of those victims would be distraught if their life styles were changed due to a global redistribution of wealth.

I wonder how many people of the American left have given thought to the consequences of fairness policies in economic markets. How much do we really care that there are people (even in the Americas) who suffer greatly and necessarily so that we might remain comfortable?

Now that Americans travel less, they will forget what little they saw of the poverty in the Third World. The fact that their comfort is the obverse of this criminal poverty doesn't seem to tarnish the brightside of the coin.

The other day, I was riding my bike through the near downtown of Las Vegas when I encountered a colony of homeless men and women. I thought about the extremes of this meeting; I, riding a bicycle that cost over $2,000 while men were sitting next to shopping carts stuffed with the detritus of a hard life on the streets. I could hardly look at them, certainly not in the eyes.

The Consumer Empire is everywhere and we are its addicts, railing at the unfairness while we consume and consume and consume. So, the question is what is the true price of the freedom? Is it our comfort?

10. Tuesday, March 23, 2004

ONCE SUSPECTED MILITARY SPY GETS REPRIMANDED FOR ADULTERY

BEWARE OF THE PEACE MAKERS
Dissembling, lying, misdirection, corruption, and other sins so extensive that even members of the Grand Old Party are outraged characterize the infamous Bush League. There are many more hot spots in the world as a result of the BL's foreign policy than before they took office.

Before Bush II, there were no terrorists in Iraq. Now the place is afoul with them. Don't forget Afghanistan and that troublesome al-Qaa'ida. They are still killing American boys and girls and hardly any media outlet reports anything more than deaths, very few comment on the failure of the BL's attempts to dismantle that organization or establish a stable government in place of the Taliban.

Do you feel safer now than you did before the BL stole the election with the open complicity of the Supreme Court? I certainly don't. As a person who has enjoyed international travel I am now reluctant to leave the country because of the violence associated with the USA and the possibility that I could be a victim of retaliatory violence.

11. Friday, March 26, 2004

BUSH JOKES ABOUT NOT FINDING WMDS IN IRAQ

WHAT DOES THIS HAVE TO DO WITH MASCOGOS?
If you've been reading this blog for any time at all, you realize that my political positions are atypical. You realize by now that I am maybe a little too pleased to be Muslim African Mascogo American (Who's your MAMA?). I can't help it; maybe its residue from the 1970's Black Pride Movement. What I do know is that I was pretty amazed to learn of my connections to the American experience stretching back to the Atlantic Slave trade and the collaborations among the indigenous folks in the Americas that made me possible.

I'm not certain how proud I should be of my ancestors who fought on the side of the colonial powers in America, even against indigenous people. What would I have done in that situation is a question that on its face is unfair to both them and me. It is the essential nature of being connected to a family history that I revel in; I am happy to see my ancestors' historical footprints because it helps to give me a sense of place. Being who I am has a context now. My physicality is explained by these known facts. My spirituality can't be far behind.

My grandmother was born at Fort Clark Seminole Camp near Brackettville, Texas. She and my mother have told me stories, actually an extended narrative although with great, interspersed silences, that comfortably merges with my imaginative skills creating a history romantically palatable and of heroic dimensions. I don't care whether the US government ever recognizes who we are or admits that they betrayed us after we helped it complete its colonization of the West. It is enough that we know it and that, like us, the knowledge of who we are and the betrayal, has fast become a part of an historical record.

Can we say never again? Yes. We must say it. We will not aid the government in its attempt to colonize African and Arab peoples; or for that matter any people. We are resident in the belly of this beast and we need to accept the responsibility of responding to it for all the voiceless. We know first hand the oppression this nation is wont to impose on others for the sake of wealth and comfort. Since we unwittingly support all of this, the responsibility to challenge it in our name and the names of the voiceless is profound. This blog is a modest attempt to that end. What does this have to do with the Mascogos? Everything.

12. Friday, April 16, 2004

IRAQ NUKE FACILITIES LEFT UNGUARDED

OSAMA, PLEASE
Yesterday in the press, Osama bin Laden is reported to have offered European nations a truce if they did not harm Muslims or Muslim nations.

Why should the West stop killing the same people he and his group kills? Muslims are not spared from his wrath even if they agree with his interpretation of Islam. We need to remember that there were Muslims killed in the attacks on the World Trade Center; there were Muslims killed in the attacks on American embassy in Kenya; and there are Muslims killed in Afghanistan. Since he proudly claims responsibility for these heinous massacres, how can he broker our well being with nations that, by the way, do not attack us so murderously direct?

I do not support the United States policies in the Middle East so don't paint my with the same brush that you paint those compromised Muslims in the United States afraid to admit the truth: the foreign policy of the United States is the policy of a nation desirous of being a fully realized empire. Even this fact, and it is a fact, does not forgive the behavior of Osama and his cohort.

I know that Osama justifies his killing of Muslims by blaming us for living in the West or being silently complicit in the wars against Muslim countries by paying taxes and generally enjoying the benefits of the Empire of Comfort. The problem with this position is that he knows, as we all know, that his country of origin is even more corrupt and oppressive than the United States and he does little, if anything, to address those wrongs. People in glass houses...

I want to make a slight digression: the struggle that faces the Western nations is not the advertised "war against terror" it is, in fact, a war against Islam. Terror, a tactical choice of certain fringe groups within the Muslim community, is a weapon. It is silly to think of a war against a weapon; the war is against those who wield the weapon. Those people are Muslim. Therefore, all Muslims are identified as the enemy of the Western nations. When he offers the Western nations an olive branch, realize that the blood of Muslims also stains that branch, and realize that we mourn his tactics, too.

13.   Friday, April 30, 2004

GEARED TO GO GAGA OVER GOOGLE

DAY DREAMING
Now that this week is coming to a close, I pray that there will not be a week like it in a very long time. Personally, things could be worse but not as disappointing as they were in terms of loss. I lost faith in my marriage. I lost a person whom I loved to cancer. The death was actually more reconcilable because she was ill with cancer for a long time. Death greets us all at the end of the day so we cannot really protest it although we may rage, rage against the dying of the light, the light inevitably dies for each of us.

I lost faith in my marriage. What does one do to recover from such a loss? She misled me on fundamental points then tried to shift the blame to me. It was that old trite argument: I did this because you did that.

The fact is I would rather be single. The lies always involved her relationships with others. She didn't lie about who squeeze the toothpaste tube from the top or whether she mailed a payment that we now find overdue; rather, she hid relationships.

This cannot be tolerated in today's social milieu. I have taken steps to get rid of the girl with the pants on fire. If you are married to someone you don't trust you are accepting into your life the disease (being ill at ease) that will define your home, and your work because things will never be right. It is, then, with thanks that this week closes.

Compared to the world's struggles, mine seem pretty small. Especially if you are a prisoner of the CPA in Iraq. You were tortured last week and probably long before then by troops supposedly sent to liberate you. That does measure up as a major deceit, doesn't it? This can't be excused by citing the "fog of war" because the war is over as per the president (you know the Crawford, Texas village idiot) when he spoke from that aircraft carrier a year ago.

14. Tuesday, May 4, 2004

EX-NSA HEAD CALLS FOR US WITHDRAWAL FROM IRAQ

FIGHTING TERROR WITH TERROR
By now, we have all seen the pictures of American soldiers abusing and torturing Iraqis in the prison, Abu Ghraib, first made infamous by Saddam Hussein. We have also learned that these soldiers were instructed to do so by inquisitors from Guantanamo Bay in Cuba where the US military is holding "suspects" from the war in Afghanistan. Rumors of torture and abuse are also leaking from that facility.

Fighting terror with terror means the terrorists have won because they created the common denominator. Furthermore, they won because they exposed the worst of America to the world. Had we abstained from barbaric responses, we would still hold the moral high ground which I believe does matter.

America looks more and more like the Evil Empire. We shame ourselves with the stain of indiscriminate violence. We were glued to our television screens as the blue-green lights exploded over Baghdad like 10,000 Fourth of Julys celebrated all at once and in another country. George the Elder would not go into Baghdad, as he knew he would be bogged down in peacekeeping and nation building.

We can play a version of the game of evil personification of the enemy in a single person (Saddam, Osama, Fidel, etc.) by blaming all of this on Bush but we have to realize that electing Kerry to the presidency will bring about little, if any, change. His words may sound sweeter but that is the sweetness borne from tasting the heartbreak of having a terrible president in the first place; it is not borne from the sweetness of a vibrant vision and will to be a better nation and a friend to those who desire to strive for change without destroying everything in their path.

I was shamed by Vietnam. I am shamed by Iraq and Afghanistan.

15. Thursday, May 13, 2004

U.S. POLL: 82% OF IRAQIS WANT U.S. OUT

AN ARGUMENT FOR THE DRAFT?
When this country abandoned the draft I was relieved because it meant that my nephews, my cousins and later my son would join the military only if they wished to serve. I understood, as we all did, that this would attract those youth who felt the military was a good upwardly mobile vehicle as well as an opportunity to travel to exotic places.

I ignored the morality of this position because it was inconvenient. However, the images from the Abu Ghraib prison still fresh, I find myself struggling to explain how those guilty of such torture and abuse, rationalize their behavior. The people in that prison were not necessarily insurgents or jihadists; many of them were victims of unlucky circumstances – being in the wrong place, being there at the wrong time.

All I can see is this army of professional killers and another army of appropriately nervous weekend warriors commonly known as the National Guard. Isn't it a wonder of our language that essentially state militias are called national? Each state has one.

The abuse appears widespread rather than being the exception. Perhaps if there were draftees, there would be less sadism.

I am wearied and ashamed. All of the killings, retaliations for killings, that horrible beheading of that young American... We seem to be straddling the abyss.

Now that the Texas village idiot has us bogged in a quagmire, he wants the UN to rescue his violent misadventure. Of course, first the UN requires that the shooting stop. Novel idea.

There is no longer the higher ground for us to stand on while we criticize the bunglers in the White House. We are waist deep in this awful muck. And here's how we can get out. Put all of the combatants in a huge mosh pit, pump up the volume, and wait to see who emerges.

Withdraw three brigades. Turn over the prisons to a civilian authority that will relinquish that authority when the new federal government is installed. Force the New Iraqi government to restore order without the assistance of US military force.

Rather than taint the new government with something from the US's shadowy history: Jim Crow and Segregation (in the form of separate but equal), the US should be in counsel with the people of Iraq with only passing attention of those charlatans who came to struggle only after Saddam had been neutralized.

Don't play the people short by seeing them as you see yourself. They will elect whom they want and those who failed to have their candidates elected can return home and come up with a better strategy.

STOP THE VIOLENCE!

16.   Wednesday, May 26, 2004

OFFICIALS WARN OF POSSIBLE MAJOR ATTACK ON US THIS SUMMER

WHEN SOVEREIGNTY AIN'T
First, let us examine the meaning of this word:
1 *obsolete*: supreme excellence or an example of it
2 a: supreme power especially over a body politic b: freedom from external control: AUTONOMY c: controlling influence
3: one that is sovereign; *especially*: an autonomous state
Autonomy. Freedom from external control. This is what we think of.

We should have understood that there was a serious breach of this concept when the Bushies began promulgating the myth of "Full Sovereignty for Iraq" which, of course, suggests that there is some other way to define sovereignty. "Full" suggests that "Partial" might be also related to sovereignty but how can there be "Partial Sovereignty"? Is it like "Partially Pregnant"? Does sovereignty suggest within its traditional usages that it can come in parcels?

This is an example of a dissembling, obfuscating administration beating a retreat from its fumbled attempt at colonizing Iraq. Now that Iraq's borders are open permitting jihadists to infiltrate the Iraqi population, now that Iraq's infrastructure needs are admitted to be greater than originally revealed, the Bushies want a way out.

There is no way to consider Iraq as sovereign nation as long as the CPA maintains its army on Iraqi soil. The big dog sleeps wherever it wants, eats whatever it desires, and kills whomever it finds offensive. What will the Iraqi government do? Will it challenge its parents, the CPA? Will it remain in hiding from its citizens waiting to see how the elections play out and whether there will be an armed struggle?

My guess is that the interim government will do exactly as it is told by the United States and Britain. When they say, "Jump!" the interim government will reply, "How high Boss? How high?"

The occupation of Iraq proved at least one point: democracy does not guarantee freedom from oppression; the American soldiers who tortured, raped and murdered Iraqis are the sons and daughters of democracy. Their oppressive acts were as heinous if not more than the ones the Iraqis suffered while Saddam was running the show because of their hypocrisy. Those soldiers committed these crimes under the cover of authority.

Democracy can morph into many forms and shapes only some of which are necessarily desirable. Besides, democracy has become the secular religion of the Western world. And like all religions, its roots are as suspect as its practices.

We must also remember that even in this so-called American democracy, that African Americans, Jews, women, and others were denied the right to vote, own property, marry freely... yet this was a democracy.

Getting out of Iraq will be difficult. I don't have the answer. Sorry. But I do know that "full sovereignty" is an evil, dissembled idea foisted on us by people who are skilled wordsmiths. The truth is that the occupation continues.

17. Thursday, June 17, 2004

9/11 PANEL: NO AL QAEDA-IRAQ 9/11LINK

RAY CHARLES
When I was a boy my parents introduced me to the music of Ray Charles Robinson. Of course, his stage name didn't include "Robinson" because he was a contemporary of Sugar Ray Robinson, the only true Sugar Ray that ever was. He didn't want to be that other Ray Robinson. He wanted to be known for his own style and achievements.

I remember singing along with him on "Drown in My Own Tears", "The Night Time is the Right Time", and "Georgia". His voice was more real to me than his lyrics. I was too young to know the pain of a lost romance or the hardship of losing a parent and my sight. So he was a hero to me because he was able to make me see pain and joy as resources that can actually power someone through a difficult time. He taught me new ways of applying the Blues.

His death certainly overshadowed the death of Saint Reagan who never authorized military interventions in Central and South America; who supported mightily the fight against HIV/AIDS; who was a friend to every disenfranchised minority; who had a memory like a safe – without the combination. Of course, everything (almost everything) that I just wrote about Saint Reagan is a big lie that is better than the dissembling the Right Wing is doing to honor him.

Saint Reagan, as he may soon be called, was incompetent. His hands are bloodied. He used the Taliban to bring the Soviet Union to its tipping point. Thanks to the stinger missiles and a dedicated rag-tag army, the USSR was forced to concede defeat that apparently was the proverbial straw or the thumb. Get it? The little Dutch boy pulled his thumb out of the dyke, and the floodwaters took the low ground then the high.

On the other hand, there's Saint Ray. And may his music lift you when you read the lies about that other guy.

18. Friday, June 18, 2004

WHITE HOUSE REASSERTS IRAQ – AL-QAEDA LINKS DESPITE 9/11 COMMISSION DEBUNKING

RAMBLINGS
Take the president of the United States. Please. We can send him to Iraq to oversee the installation of the colonial government that is being clumsily disguised as a sovereign state.

Did anyone other than me wonder about the hypocrisy of the United States when it declared that it would ensure the proportional distribution of power in Iraq be based on ethnic and religious affiliations? Why don't we do that here? If Latinos (whatever a Latino is) are 12 percent of the population, give them 12 percent of the seats in Congress. If Jews are 2 percent, give them 2 percent.

And since we know African Americans are not going to get a fair shake in this country, give us a separate state (I'll take California). Then give us the option of relocation and temporary subsidies. I'm certain we can hammer out an immigration law with Mexico that will ensure the fair treatment of its citizens.

So now Madonna is neo-Jewish? She's into the Cabbala. I remember a rabbi told me that once the outward was the outward and the inward, the inward but today the outward has become inward and the inward has become outward. By this he meant to convey that prayers and other rituals that were once outward signs of faith have become considered mystical while the mystical dimensions, at least the outer husks, are being sold in candy stories everywhere. Thus: Madonna (Esther).

Bush's policy of preemptive strikes gives me another idea. I consider Bush a threat to my peace, should I therefore... never mind. I support adherence to international law. What a novel idea. In the community of nations, we should acknowledge the community's interests in maintaining productive relationships within it as well as disincentives to act unilaterally.

19. Wednesday, June 23, 2004

BUSH CLAIMED RIGHT TO IGNORE GENEVA CONVENTIONS

MISSISSIPPI GODDAMN
Yesterday someone in passing mentioned that Nevada was called the Mississippi of the West. He was explaining to me the explicit racism that I was running into regularly at one of Las Vegas' poser educational institutions. Of course, the operative word is "was" because nowhere in the United States is racism so pervasive and destructive these days as it was in the days in which Emmet Till was lynched because he "looked" at a white woman.

I remember the picture of his battered body as it appeared in Jet Magazine. I was only 10 years old at the time and it frightened me to the extent that I have absolute flawless recall of that picture and the circumstances that produced it.

They want to put the alleged perpetrator on trial. Finally, justice may be rendered but I can't help but say, "Justice delayed is justice denied." I am 58 years old. African Americans and others who did not meet the archetype American citizen have experienced delayed justice on so many fronts that now, in the shadows of that era, we all know that justice has been denied us.

As our friends in victimization say, "Never again."

20. Tuesday, June 29, 2004

QUESTIONS RAISED OVER MISSING IRAQI MONEY

A LESSON IN ABROGATION
When I became a Muslim it was necessary for me to learn Arabic so that I could read the Qur'an with understanding and recite it properly. I knew enough of what Islam was to embrace it without reservation but I felt it was necessary to go beyond trust in the translations of the Qur'an and the interpretations of friends.

That was a seminal decision as many important life experiences emanated from it. I learned the language through formal study and earned a masters degree from the University of Michigan. Reading the Qur'an can take one in many directions. I began to search for its structure, for the rudiments of the formative verses that led to ruminations on the jurisprudential issues rather than the manifestation of its results in the Shari'a or formalized Islamic law.

Eventually, I came face-to-heart with the concept of "Naskh" or abrogation. This occurs in the Qur'an when one verse either cancels or, more likely, modifies a previously revealed verse. The problem with this concept should be apparent. If Allah were All Knowing, why would it ever be necessary to alter His Word? Does not this abrogating verse say, in effect, that He did not get it right the first time?

I am certain that the concept of abrogation has led to many issues, especially indirectly, that have challenged the faith of some and humanized the Deity in ways that are too close to what we call "Shirk" or associating others with Allah.

At first, to defend myself from internal dissolution, I denied that abrogation ever occurred in the Qur'an. I found a few scholars that agreed with this position but it required ignoring some pretty blatant examples of it. Eventually, I put it out of my conscious mind because I could not end the discussion in any acceptable way.

Then I began to envision abrogation as one of the most important aspects of the revelatory process. The Qur'an, it must be noted, contains guidance on how to be a Muslim by describing processes, four in number, all derived from a central idea: the confession of faith, "I witness that there is nothing deserving of worship except Allah and I witness that Muhammad is the messenger of Allah". This declaration is the fundament from which the four pillars emerge. To use a tentmaker's metaphor: the Bearing of Witness is the center pole of the tent while the other 4: ritual prayer, ritual fasting, alms giving, and the ritual pilgrimage to Makka hold up the tent nearer its edges, in clear view of others. Allah only sees the center pole. Even the believer is blind to the condition of his center pole until the believer reaches the status of "knowing". I embraced the concept that the Qur'an teaches us processes by which we can begin to "know" by leading us to the five prayers, to Ramadan, to zakat, and to the hajj which are the pathway and price.

I submit that by embracing the concept of abrogation, we learn that Allah acknowledges change in how we are to express our beliefs, not in any fundamental sense but to refine our actions so that we might improve our behavior toward our families, our communities, and our nations.

This call for replacing a blessing with a bigger blessing will disturb the Wahhabis and their cousins but why else would Allah abrogate His words if not to teach us the importance of embracing not only change but also the need to change?

21. Friday, July 9, 2004

U.S. MILITARY: IRAQI RESISTANCE CAN'T BE MILITARILY DEFEATED

HOW LONG HAS THE TRAIN BEEN GONE?
This is the bewilderment, helpless as much as it is hapless, of a man who has missed the train. This is the mournful cry of a man who missed his train and doesn't yet know how he will make the necessary arrangements to get where he ought to be.

There was something worthwhile about getting aboard that train that he will forever forgo. It could be his professional career. It could be the love of his life. It could be the chance to escape life's futility.

On the other hand, it could be a cry of relief or thanksgiving. His sworn enemy, he knows for certain, was on that train.

His wife was on that train so he now, at ease, can lay with his lover.

The men who were looking for him have retreated to their Chicago dungeons and he is now forever free of their claims.

The fact that the train is gone can be a cause for celebration and remorse. Opportunities can be fleeting. It is necessary to take full advantage of what the train might offer while it is in the station or, having boarded her, while she is underway.

Dubya missed the opportunity to become a statesman with his invasion of Iraq. People could see his purpose in invading Afghanistan; after all, Osama was there. Iraq? Iraq was a toothless tiger with no spring in its step. Dubya and his posse went so far as to make certain that those illegal missiles were destroyed before ordering the troops to attack

He missed the Statesman Line as it rolled across the White House lawn. Missing that train means he can't possibly get on board now.

John F Kerry and John Edwards can catch a train to the White House because Dubya is so inadequate that even members of his party know he has to go. But will they? JFK and JE are not exactly setting a pace that Dubya can't match. I think that if they are to win, they have to engage those voters who are afraid that by changing leadership the wrong message is sent to America's sworn enemies.

How long has the train been gone? Longer, perhaps, than you know.

22. Friday, July 23, 2004

RUMSFELD SET EYES ON IRAQ AT 2:40 PM SEPT. 11, 2001

RAMBLINGS
- I have been wondering, nearly aloud, about what will happen to this nation, being so embittered toward other nations. Will this bitterness become blowback expressed as more acts of terror?

    These concerns are heightened dramatically by what the Bushies believe to be the only policy that can save America from the terrorist hordes: preemptive strikes. They, as intellectually challenged and morally corrupt as they are, might use Iraq as an example of the success of that strategy.

    You may stop laughing now.

- Have we forgotten Afghanistan? Is this not the country that calls the mayor of Kabul its president? A president, mind you, hand picked by the most active of all the neo-colonial states but who is out-muscled by warlords and the remnants of the Taliban. Elections are scheduled for October. Could this schedule be in deference to Bush, Karzai's true boss?

- Lance Armstrong is going to win his 6th Tour de France. What hard work and dedication he has demonstrated, shaming all of us who are quasi-committed to our lives' goals. Wake up. Dedication, hard work, and serendipity will get it done. No promises. Just opportunities.

- We have a presidential race that is plump with opportunity for sexual jokes. We have a Dick hiding inside a Bush Whitehouse trying to outsmart two Johns. Both Johns wanted to beat the Bush but Edwards agreed Kerry should go first. Dick is flaccid and the Bush is witless. But where they sit is truly seductive so one John looks forward to beating Dick while the other lusts for the Bush seat.

23. Wednesday, July 28, 2004

FLORIDA REVEALS IT LOST ELECTRONIC VOTING ECORDS

BARACK OBAMA...
Today, in Slate, MSN's online magazine, the author Saletan did a piece on Barack Obama. In it he mentions Obama's African dad and white American mom and decided that Barack was not exactly black. This blew me away.

Saletan has shown his ignorance of the American definition of black. If you have a black parent in America you are black. It doesn't matter whether your other parent is aboriginal (read: Native American), Asian, Indian, or whatever. You are black.

He should know this. Most of us considered African Americans are varied and multi-hued. We have African, First Nations, and European heritages merging in our gene pool. Just look at us. You can see the proof on our faces, in our eyes, in our hair and you can hear it in our voices.

We, as a people, are as close as America has come to stirring the mythic melting pot. You do not get more genetically American than us.

However, racism continues to define how we label groups. We have Latinos who are also represented as Africans, First Nations and Europeans. In their cases, however, the Europeans were Spanish speakers. On the faces of Latinos you can see the African, the aboriginal, the European. But they are conveniently dismissed as Latinos as if that expression explains everything about their origin and history.

And Jews. Are they white? Some, yes. Others, no. But our categorization is driven by the need to garner all of the uncertainties that have a favorable spin associated with them under the rubric of white (except when the doors are closed and the anti-Semitism is allowed expression).

Saletan is putting a spin on Barack Obama because he likes him. He wants him in his tent because he is an articulate, educated man with much political promise. If he were a purse-snatcher or gang-banger, he would not hesitate to call him African American.

To Obama's credit, he does not slink from his identity. He fully embraces his history and accepts the classification of African American imposed on him because he understands America's need to categorize racially. I bet he also knows that race is a pseudo-scientific concept that continues to rationalize how we view others and ourselves.

Saletan, you need to wake up. Obama, in his own words, fully and proudly embraces the term African American.

Yes. For better or for worse, he is my brother. If he proves to be the good man that he appears to be, maybe we should make him an honorary Mascogo. We, too, are a complex mixture of peoples.

24.   Thursday, August 5, 2004

NUCLEAR POWER PLANT SAFETY LAPSES NO LONGER PUBLIC

WHEN IT'S BAD
I got married almost a year ago. This wasn't my first time. I should have known better. The thing is most of us get plenty of warnings before we do it but rarely do we actually heed those warnings. Guilty am I.

That cold feeling? That elaborate distance?

I went ahead. The coldness turned to drizzle then sleet then snow. The snow began soft and flaky. Then it was beady and hard. Then it came fiercely, borne by the wicked nor'easter sailors bemoan.

That elaborate distance took on the sanctity of a woman's right not to communicate. The right to be quiet and aloof was born the instant Eve slipped out of Adam's side.

She, the woman I married said her mother had trouble hugging her own kids. Some legacy. The theme of distance and aloofness is a more conclusive part of my gestalt than I could have ever imagined. The lack of intimacy blooms a rotting flower.

25. Friday, August 27, 2004

36 MILLION NOW IN POVERTY; 45 MILLION UNINSURED

ABU GHURAIB: THE FATHER OF YOUR CONTEMPTUOUS ABSENCE AND ESTRANGEMENT

People have been wondering aloud, especially on public radio (where the commentators actually are provided enough time to make meaningful comments), about the meaning and pronunciation of this phrase. NPR's "All Things Considered" did an admirable job on the pronunciation part by broadcasting actual Iraqis repeating the phrase. However, ATC did stumble on the meaning.

Idiomatic expressions are essentially untranslatable and we should look for phrases that convey similar ideas rather than literally translating an idiom. "Abu", for example, may convey fatherhood, source, ownership, etc.

"Ghraib" is derived from the trilateral root GH R B. This root yields the word "maGHRiB" which we translate as "West".

"GHuRaiB" presents a vowel pattern that is associated with the diminutive. The diminutive can take on a variety of meanings including enhancement and contempt. The ability for one word or phrase to have contradictory meanings is actually common.

The definition of "GHaRaB" is "strange, depart, leave, etc." When colored by the diminutive, and preceded by "Abu" it can mean the "Father of your Contemptuous Absence" which does sound like a good name for a prison. This phrase has nothing to do with the West although ATC thought it might.

WHAT IS WRONG WITH JOHN KERRY

First, why would anyone base a political campaign for the highest office in the land on four months in Vietnam? I am a Vietnam era person who did not want to go to that war because, on its face, it was immoral. I thought so then and I think so now. There is no moral high ground to be seized by those who chose to go there and kill people fighting for their right to self-determination.

Of all the things Bush has said and done, Kerry doesn't appear willing to challenge him on them. This makes me wonder whether he is silent because he, if elected, would do the same things. We face a huge deficit; we are crazy with fear of terrorism; we are at "war" with a tactic and not a nation or a group; and the numbers of the poor have been increasing throughout his administration.

LIAR, LIAR PANTS ON FIRE!
Bushites lied against a triple amputee who lost his limbs in the Vietnam War, placing his picture next to Osama and Saddam and questioned his patriotism; Bushites lied against a present US senator who suffered for 5 years in a POW camp in Vietnam, questioning his loyalty and patriotism. Why are we surprised that they are doing the same thing against Kerry? After all, Bush is no flip flopper, he.

THE RELUCTANT JIHADIST

26.   Monday, October 18, 2004

GOP THREATENS GROUP NOT TO DISCUSS THE
POSSIBILITY OF A DRAFT

IT'S BEEN A LONG TIME BUT THERE'S GOING TO BE A CHANGE
I've been in a general malaise. I've been distracted by the noise emanating from the campaign trails of two incompetents begging for attention as they both try an act as if they are not incompetent.

Bush versus Kerry is a little like Fric versus Frac; it's a coin toss as they represent two sides of the same dross covered coin. Heads or tails? It doesn't matter too much because whichever way it lands it is still only a penny. Okay, Bush is more obviously a manipulated marionette but Kerry, stiff and wrinkled as a used cloth dropped behind the clothes hamper, doesn't have any credibility even with the people who despise his opponent.

I use to ride without a helmet. One day, I decided, on a lark really, to wear it. There was no special reason. I wasn't racing. I wasn't even planning to extend myself that much as it should have been a recovery day. Going downhill at 27 MPH, I hit a patch of uneven concrete (yes concrete, not asphalt); over corrected my front wheel and crashed.

At least I was able to land on my left side, thus avoiding smashing my derailleur. But I landed on my hip, arms and head. The helmet did several things admirably. It distributed effectively the force of the impact; it kept my neck from overextending; and then it took the force of my head hitting, face forward. Okay, the rest of me looked like hamburger. I tore a collector's jersey; ripped the backside of my gloves; and scratched my wedding band badly. I bought another helmet even before I was physically able to ride again.

Ramadan has begun. Thirty days of fasting, praying, assessing. As the world turns its attention to the business of this emerging great cultural war between Western Christianity and Radical Muslim

Sectarianism, America reaches for the flag of leadership. The problem is that it is very difficult for a state, saddled with slow moving, anti-intellectual activism to address a decentralized, very mobile group of Radical Muslim Sectarians. This is especially true when the state is not competent in defining the battleground or even the issues on which this conflict rests.

27. Thursday, November 18, 2004

SENATE OKS DEBT CEILING TO REACH $8.2 TRILLION

IT HAS BEEN AWHILE
The president was reelected, Iraq continued to burn while the rest of the world imitated Nero, and the so-called religious right grew more disrespectful of their religion and of our rights of dissent.

Bush talks about his reelection giving him new capital to pursue his policies and stating that he will spend that capital. The fact is, however, that capital is to be invested in a manner that the real stockholders gain, not the egocentric views of the chief executive. It should not be spent unless, of course, you are a corporate raider looking for coffers to fleece and sneak away while the investors cry over their losses.

Candi Rice as the new secretary of state? Could he have done worse? Yeah. But not easily. Did he say, "What would Jesus do" before announcing or did it come to him in a morning prayer session (after she rose from the altar and swallowed)?

There are more and more Americans leaving the country as a result of the presidential election. They are fleeing into Canada as the once great Cree Nation did, as the victims of American slavery once did. Canada has been the refuge of America's oppressed for centuries. If you haven't been there, you should visit because it is truly a different place, spiritually and politically. Canadians are more peaceful and socially conscious.

Maybe Bush should invade Canada. The Canadians oppose his foreign policy. Their domestic policies are too liberal to even be discussed by the US legislators. Their drugs are cheaper. They don't play baseball very well. He could always enlist "Team America". Check this movie out. Inspired puppet sex.

And Mexico is too important to the economies of the Southwest to bother the Mexicans. Think about this: while you're removing your shoes and having your undies examined by minimum wage badges,

Mexicans and Central Americans are coming across the border basically unobstructed at the rate of over 4,000 a day. Now, what door would you be watching? The one where citizens are transiting from one state to another or where non-citizens are penetrating your border? It depends, finally, on your political and financial interests.

Now about those Muslims. America has sprouted Muslims who, by their lack of backbone and principles, essentially either endorse Bush's policies or remain quiet lest they be thought of as embracing terrorism. So they go to the White House, grinning. This is especially true for the so-called immigrant community. If you were to look at their demographics, you'd think you were looking at Republicans and Democrats. If you were to stand next to them in prayer you'd notice that many of them couldn't see their feet because of their expansive bellies. No one should worry about terrorists among this group.

28. Thursday, January 13, 2005

MARGARET THATCHER'S SON SENTENCED IN AFRICAN COUP PLOT

I GUESS I'M LAZY
I read Bob Dylan's, "Chronicles: Volume 1". This is a must read for every one old enough to read.

Just yesterday, the Bush administration let it be known, in the softest voice discernible in network news, that it was closing its search in Iraq for weapons of mass destruction. They let it be known however, that he would have done it anyway... which is to say, he did it anyway. I don't believe that anyone, except those in the Blood (red) States, really thought that WMD's were their or that Saddam was really giving stuff to Crazy Muslims (whom he also feared). But he did try to kill his daddy. If someone tried to kill my daddy, I'd kick his ass, too.

Let's see: civil war looming in Iraq, opium blooming in Afghanistan... Seems to me somebody's report card is not too good. But John Kerry's wasn't too good either. He tried to out-Bush Bush. Nothing is ever as good or as bad as the original. He was a toothless tiger whose tongue slid aimlessly from one side of his mouth to the other. But I voted. I, like many, voted against Bush in total futility. War presidents need to be retired. What we need is a Peace president smart enough to help peace along. Of course, there's no president able to bring peace to the Middle East (what, exactly is it in the middle of anyway, except a big old mess?). But at least he could give everybody cash directly instead of spending billions on munitions that just kill or piss everybody off.

How about the rains? It rained so hard in Los Angeles, that I thought I was standing under fireman's hose... something like the Southern wrath of the fifties and sixties without Bull Connor directing it at colored folks.

Mascogos: don't worry that the Seminoles don't want to cut us in. Don't worry the BIA doesn't want to recognize us. All we have to worry about is ensuring that we don't forget who we are.

I am troubled by the role we played in the killing and imprisonment of indigenous people. We were excellent scouts and brave warriors and the US would have won anyway but our role isn't necessarily something to brag about although it is something to remember. Because after all we did to help the US, they betrayed us, too. The Euro-Americans hold their religion and their constitution behind their backs to be used whenever it is convenient. They don't live their religion; they use it to fool and conquer people. The constitution was written with only white men in mind.

29. Thursday, March 31, 2005

CHILD MALNUTRITION RATE DOUBLES IN IRAQ POST-INVASION

RADICAL SUNNA?
The perspective that many Muslims hold regarding the place of the Sunna of the Prophet Muhammad is rationalized by referring to the verse in the Qur'an in which Allah says that He has perfected the religion. Perfection, this point of view holds, cannot accept innovations, as they would cause what is now perfect to become imperfect.

The early Muslim community, however, did not embrace this argument, as it faced many unique challenges in bringing the practices of the prophet into dynamic world arenas. Many Muslims excuse these changes with the caveat that the innovators had close relationships with the prophet and these were less than changes and more like enhancements and clarifications rightly guided them.

These same Muslims argue that the Qur'an contains verses that were abrogated by other verses. These abrogations, they hold, represent refinements rather than changes and reflect the spiritual and political growth of the Muslim community. They do not perceive these abrogations as contrary to the notion of perfection but rather as one of the mechanisms to achieve it.

I would like to present a different view of the "perfection" verse and the role of the Sunna in the lives of Muslims. It is clear that some verses in the Qur'an are meant as abrogations of other verses as well as abrogations of Sunnatic practices. This dynamism is, in effect, a respected part of the Sunna but, I believe, is misapplied. The abrogating nature of these verses suggested to me at one point that the Qur'an was imperfect in that it appeared to be a work in progress rather than a Recitation created before time.

Could it be that these verses import is more related to the process than the outcome? In other words, was Allah teaching humanity that adaptation to the changing condition of humanity was appropriate in the same manner that He adapted the Qur'an without compromising its integrity? It occurred within the practices of the people of Medina. It occurred within the practice of the prophet and the earliest community.

Of course, I am not suggesting changing the Qur'an; I am suggesting changing the behaviors of Muslims. The fact that women were not permitted the same weight legally as men may have been appropriate given certain conditions. It is important, in this context, to acknowledge that some women of those times owned more weight legally than men. For example, those women who knew the prophet played an unequalled role in the preservation of the Sunna as well as the Qur'an. Therefore, it is not as if women were judged to be inferior; perhaps there status at that time was generally inferior but not their nature.

Applying this logic to the development of community mores allows for the abandonment of practices that are obviously archaic and inappropriate. Additionally, it frees us from the residual affects of extra-Sunnatic practices (purdah, circumcision – male and female, the head to toe covering of women, for examples).

We can formulate a methodology in a manner that presents the primary source, the Qur'an, as the basis for our actions. This methodology could embrace, after contextualization, the practices of the first and second-generation Muslims of Medina.

We need to free ourselves from the false notion that the Qur'an and Sunna are perfect systems. The perfection lies in knowing why, when and how to adapt to the world.

THE RELUCTANT JIHADIST

30. Monday, April 25, 2005

U.S. PRISON POPULATION REACHES 2.1 MILLION

PAPA WAS A ROLLING STONE
The pope was a rolling stone. He loved to travel. This may have given the Catholic Church a higher profile but I doubt that he did it for pleasure or that we need to make any kind of fun of him for his predilection for foreign ports.

People have mourned his death but unless I slept through it, it doesn't seem like people cared a great deal about what he had to say which leads me to conclude that the people didn't know the meaning of the Vicar of Christ or they didn't care. It has been quite a long time (in human terms) since Jesus is supposed to have died.

Anyway, now we have an ex-Hitler Youth and Nazi soldier holding down the job. This alone is telling. His brother is reported to have said, "What else could we have done?" when queried about why they became tools in the Nazi's war against humanity. The fact that he deserted when the Third Reich was about to fall is not heartwarming; it speaks, probably, to the same accommodative attitude that saw him join in arms with the devil in the first place.

The Americans won't let Baathists hold any substantial position in the new Iraq but then turn and praise the ex-Nazi pope. What gives?

As far as the doctrinal issues go, both John Paul and Benedict stand for the things that have become known as Roman Catholicism. I don't get why so many are upset with this. No belief based in what is believed to be sacred knowledge direct from the Almighty can change to accommodate the topical. The question arises: did the Almighty have a change of heart? I can hear it from above:

"Did I say my priests are not to marry? I've changed my mind! Since you failed to implement it across the board (you know about the Greek Orthodox, right?), I'm changing my eternal all-knowing mind. Besides, the Mother Irony of all ironies, you are outdoing the Greeks with your utter fascination with little boys."

Even as popular as John Paul II was, the masses didn't want to listen to his homilies. He was like the nice but doting great grandfather. You smiled as you listened to him prattling gibberish, spittle seeping from the corners of his mouth and that one thickened ball of spittle glued to the medial-peak of his upper lip, being stretched by the connectivity of his bottom lip every time he sucked air to empower his next nonsensical phrase.

But since he was family and gentle with that cherubic mien surfacing now and then, you look forward to seeing him. When he wanders (or wonders for that matter) off, we all search madly for him because we love him; we just don't listen to him.

But now we got this guy who had no choice but to become a Nazi (until it was clear who was actually going to win the war) running a church that raptures over saints (at least a few of whom were sainted because of their refusal to serve the devil).

I am so not supportive of this hypocrisy. It's not like this Benny is terrible for having made substantial mistakes in his life as a youth but some mistakes disqualify one from achieving certain positions.

And now we find out that he wanted to hide the investigations off child molesters disguised as priests. Cynicism.

31. Friday, June 24, 2005

KKK LEADER SENTENCED TO 60 YEARS FOR 1964 KILLINGS

AN INELEGANT LENGTHY ABSENCE
I've been putting approximately 115 miles a week on my bike but I can't lose the troubles. They seem to be permanently in my slipstream. Perhaps I'll slow down and then suddenly increase my speed, especially if there's a climb looming ahead, and drop them like Michael dropped the gun in the Godfather.

THE ABROGATING (NAASIKH) AND THE ABROGATED (MANSUUKH)
It is well established in the Qur'anic sciences that later verses abrogated various earlier ones. It is also established that the Qur'an for example, abrogated some practices of the prophet, of which some were borrowings from Judaism - the Stoning.

I had a very difficult time integrating this concept with the concept that Allah revealed the Qur'an because I couldn't fathom why the Omniscient One would ever have a change of heart (excuse the anthropomorphism).
That particular struggle ended when I theorized that it was not a contradiction because the perfection of the Recitation (that's what 'Qur'an means) resides not in its immutability but in its processes.

Perfection represents the antithesis to life because once perfection is realized all that follows is imperfection. Allah, my theory says, presented us with an open system as a perfect model for embracing change. Sometimes the change is revealed in the hearts of Muslims, sometimes change is guided by the best minds of the community. One change in Saudi Arabia does not necessarily require the same change in the United States.

The fundamental rituals do not change, as ritualized behavior is really what binds the community together. Rarely do you know the sociopolitical thought of the person next to you during prayer. What you do know is that you are completing a required ritual. If you are observant, you may notice the positioning of the hands (and sundry other details) during the ritual that will inform you what Way (School) he follows. The calcification of thought that the Schools represent has not served us well and certainly is contrary to the theory I am articulating.

Think of the possibilities.

32.   Friday, July 22, 2005

MOUNT ST. HELENS STILL SHAKING

AND THE TIMES... ARE THEY CHANGIN'?
I was listening to Bob Dylan sing this anthem the other day as I rode through Griffith Park. I did note some changes but none so remarkable to render song writing appropriate.

Well, there're still the wars (Afghanistan, Iraq, Palestine, Darfur, etc.). No change there.

Bush is still stumbling over his next words. Same old. Same old.

The people of the West and the people of the East continue to pretend that they are not on a collision course right there in the seas of cultural change. They each feel that it is okay to kill the other for the greater good. The problem, of course, is that whose greater good will be determined ultimately by who has the best killing machines.

Well... Back in the 1970's some said make love and not war but I think many think that war is actually more fun. You ever see men train as hard for sex as they do for war?

Besides, make enough babies and you'll have to go to war to feed them.

33. Monday, July 25, 2005

WHITE HOUSE LOBBIES GOP SENATORS NOT TO PASS ANTI-TORTURE BILL

THANK YOU, LANCE
I've always loved cycling. I don't know whether it was simply moving so freely so quickly, a sky blue canopy, manicured lawns, explorations, or just the road.

I can remember learning to ride on my aunt's full sized bicycle when I could not have been older than five or six years. Conveniently, it was a traditional girls' bike with no crossbar.

My parents encouraged me more by giving me what we called an "English Racer". I rode that bike all over the neighborhood.

I took up riding more seriously in 1974. I purchased a Japanese bike branded Centurion Super Le Mans (I think) and rode faithfully all over Detroit. I often put in 4-hour rides after work and longer rides on the weekend.

I took this bike with me to Philadelphia and rode that town for a year. Philly was a great bike town. Maybe it was the fact that there was a tradition of messenger bikes that created such a tolerant atmosphere.

I took that same bike to Indianapolis and rode there, too. However, when I moved to Los Angeles, I had to hang the bike up, literally. LA was a mean city to ride. After several years of fighting angry drivers, I sold the bike and turned to basketball. I was never very good in basketball but during this phase, my skills certainly improved.

After surrendering my bike and tiring of basketball, I bought a pair of Roller Blades. This led to eventually purchasing a rather high end set up (Riedell boots, Labeda rails, the largest and hardest wheels and the best bearings. I actually became pretty fast but I missed cycling.

Finally, and retrospectively probably influenced by all the attention given cycling because of Lance Armstrong's incredible story, I came back to cycling. Cycling has become a big part of my identity. I bought an entry-level road bike (Cannondale CAAD 5 R700). This was a good place to start because it was inexpensive although that was due to the second tier componentry that came with it. Eventually, I upgraded it with the Dura Ace group and Kysirium wheels. The bike loss four pounds and I gained a bunch of speed.

I even managed to ride two summers in Las Vegas. I had to ride at night to avoid the scorching sun but it was still usually quite hot (hovering around 100 degrees). If you ever go to Las Vegas, you have to ride Red Rock Canyon. It is a ride with nice challenges and beautiful vistas.

Now I own a Cannondale Six13. My skills have grown and I am a much better cyclist now. Lance, of course, was right when he wrote, "Its not about the Bike". It isn't. To know what it is about, you've got to ride.

So, on the occasion of his last professional ride, I thank Lance for reinvigorating cycling in the US.

And if you care enough about what I have to say to have read this far, go out and buy yourself a decent bike and ride, Sally, ride!

34. Thursday, July 28, 2005

BUSH DECLARES AN END TO PHRASE 'WAR ON TERROR'

FEAR AND MOBILITY
I've decided not to travel abroad. Fear can do that.

I guess the American government has seen enough of me now to realize that I am not a threat to the peace and security of my extended family, many friends and fellow citizens so I am no longer obstructed from traveling.

I am no longer pulled aside for another level of personal identification. Right after the attack of September-11-2001, I stopped flying because I was hassled by airport security. Well, maybe they knew that I have traveled in Africa and the Middle East as well as having an Arabic name and passing acquaintances with persons that our government probably considers terrorists.

Foreign governments would probably admit me (I have done nothing wrong people, and I am not planning to do anything wrong). But the media has convinced me that I should wait a little while before going back to Africa or the Middle East. I do want to go to Asia but that's another story.

I have, let's say, a friend whose life is being defined by her fears to a much greater extent. She willingly lives in substandard housing; her fear of being found to be inadequate has frozen her in a dead-end job. She fears change although she's smart enough to realize that change is constant. She thinks of it as an enemy to be avoided which means by the time change is on her, it does, in effect, victimize her again.

I work with a woman who is disabled by a history of abuse (drugs, spousal) and a very poor education. She's surrendered the possibility of shaping the change that is inevitably happening all around her. Thus, she is suspicious of everything.

These, son, are three examples of debilitating fear. Each is an example of fear resulting in various expressions of immobility. Frozen by fear, change rolls over us like an ocean wave over sandbars. Although the sandbars may have other intentions, each wave will transform some aspect of its *sandbar-ness*. Living so close to the ocean means that I know that sometimes waves contain harmful things ranging from stinging jellyfish to human waste.

I try to encourage these women to act despite of their fear because the act itself is empowering and will lead to reactions and other actions. Most of what we do when attempting to neutralize our fears is to take "baby steps". This maybe a good thing because small victories do build confidence and as confidence increases based, the next disappointments take on a different hue: we see balance and not victimization.

Go for it. One step at a time. The key: keep stepping.

35. Friday, August 5, 2005

CHEVRON PAYS NIGERIAN SOLDIERS ALLEGED TO HAVE KILLED VILLAGERS

SURPRISES
Surprise No. 1
Now that the war against terror is over and we are now engaged in the Global Struggle Against Violent Extremists, we should feel a little relieved. There. It's done! G SAVE. That could mean, in other environs, Gangsta SAVE. That might be even more appropriate.

Surprise No. 2
Besides, things are looking rather bleak for the Bush in Afghanistan and Iraq. Al-Qaa'ida is raising hell in Afghanistan and Pakistan with political assassinations and over-running military bases in Afghanistan.

Surprise No. 3
We have Bush to thank for the increase in opium production in Afghanistan. Production is up since its pacification and the installment of the new, democratic regime. Karzai can't leave the capital without American soldiers guarding him and even then things are apt to get dicey.

Surprise No. 4
I've heard that the insurgents (are they now violent extremists or terrorists -- I'm a little confused) particularly like to attack the national guardsmen rather than the regular army because success is much more likely. Whatever the case, Bush is taking a beating there and, from all indications, a civil war is looming as large as a new moon near the horizon.

Surprise No. 5
The Supreme Court Nominee once did important pro bono work for the gay rights movement resulting in a landmark decision by the Supreme Court. Neo-cons are bouncing off the wall. He went to an all boys' school, played Peppermint Patty in a school play. He didn't

marry until he was 41 (some hint his marriage was politically motivated). The Christian Right is agog with confusion.

Appointing a homosexual to the Supreme Court may, in effect, give it some balance. We know we already have a justice with a history of obsession with pornography. Does being gay mean he cannot be a good judge? Being gay puts him outside the mainstream but it does not make him odd or irreligious. I think pornography, at least in our time, is very mainstream yet very hidden. Homosexuals are partially out but fans of pornography are closeted.

36. Friday, August 26, 2005

TYPHOON MAWAR HITS JAPAN, AT LEAST ONE DEAD, TWO MISSING, FOUR INJURED

SONG FOR MY FATHER
Horace Silver gave us this music some time ago and every time I hear it I think of my father who, to this day, his children call, "Daddy". Our parents took care of us. We were well fed, clothed, and received excellent health care the entire time they were responsible for us.

They went further. We were encouraged to play music, read, participate in sports, go to camps, and many other activities.

He was there to guide me through juvenile delinquency never giving up on me; and I had some big problems.

We hear about African American fathers being absent but that was not the case with our family. He worked hard. Made certain that we learned how to work hard. All of their children are college graduates but we all have blue-collar souls.

My Dad taught me mathematics when the public schools couldn't. He taught me to drive. He was not always a patient parent but when he was teaching me these important skills, he was patient and understanding. He kept the goal and my self-esteem in mind.

Now, my father is dying. The polio he overcame as a youth returned with a vengeance none of us expected. And this tribulation has become the stage on which he teaches us how to die. He has maintained high spirits, facing his obvious situation with humor and dignity. He thanks god for not having much pain, rather than complaining about the pain he does have.

37.   Monday, September 12, 2005

REPORT: 1,500 CHILDREN STILL SEPARATED FROM
PARENTS AFTER HURRICANE

A SONG FOR MY FATHER

> The Unworlding°
> UAH/9/9/2005

The funereal days were languorously beautiful
Brimming, hour after hour, embarrassingly
Brightful sun filled days:
This state of ecological near-grace
Mollifies our blues.

> While Katrina Huracan revels in her fury, revealing
> Fraudulence, pestilence, nonchalance, and incompetence:
> The four American horsemen of the bush-apocalypse.
> Waves breaching levees, tornadoes roaring, hailstones slamming

> Bodies swelling with death's effluence,
> Gas-bloated carcasses drifting, darkened cityscapes drowned -
> There was no Rapture; only death and fear
> For the poor souls abandoned by a military
> state at war.

We walked into the church, birthright aware,
While family and friends were restive in rows
Oh Danny boy, the pipes are calling –
I thought about candied sweet potatoes

Days of summer:
Ash bats driving fastballs back, back... and
Stretching singles in the late innings;
Shaking off signs. Coming with sliders and sometimes heat

> It is the poor souls who cling to roofs
> While toxic waters roil and rise to choke off their protests.

Their lives hidden within the myth of the city as jazz cool,
Their accents mellifluous, African rhythms, French melodies, Indian
sage.

Locked down in sports arenas
For their own good; protection from armed terrorists
Government banned cameras and official denials of responsibility
Because the buck can't stop there– its romping wild, lost in the Iraqi
desert.

Armfuls of sadness wrapped around our shoulders
Burdened twice now, by our own grief and now theirs;
Kisses dampening our cheeks, our minds racing through
Darkened halls of neglected memories for clues:

Who owns this face, familiar and then not or not
And then familiar; eyes glancing blows across their face
Trying desperately to authenticate a recollection:
Yes! I know who you are, and without difficulty.

She heard the people who live below
Clawing the ceiling and gasping for air;
The waters ripped her from his hand
As she pled, sped away by the roiling flood, for him to care for their
child.

The waters are streaked with rainbows
Gas stations, dry cleaners, DuPont:
All surrender their toxicity to the memory of Katrina
Huracan, the merciless angel whose wings powered this fury.

Children can see their fathers' invisibles:
Flaws, more than the better angels, of his nature:
All entangled mercilessly, Bramble bushes and razor grasses,
Punctuated by oases of compassion, grace, and forgiveness.

We observe others from the acute angles of our prejudices;
Our fears, born of sins, real and imagined, persist in the deeds of others

THE RELUCTANT JIHADIST

We imagine our fathers as us, acting on our motives
Because they must fear what we fear as we fear only what is real.

> *The waters continued to rise amorally.*
> *The poor drown more equally than the rich.*
> *No pictures. No pictures. You are to take no pictures.*
> *Rats are eating the gas-bloated*
> *rigor mortis floating corpus.*

Our invigorated clan witnesses the unworlding of my father.
He travels the Milky Way as the Mascogos who have gone before him.
May he be in the peace, of the peace, the peace itself.
May we walk in good relation to the earth, in peace and bravery.

38.   Friday, October 21, 2005

TOM DELAY GETS BOOKED, SMILES IN MUG SHOT

THE ONLY TRULY WORTHWHILE QUESTION
First, let us assume that there is a knowing god who is omniscient, omnipotent, and loving. Having accepted this rather Western view of the divine that includes god acting intelligently as a creator, teacher, awarder, punisher, and killer of human souls, we create a meaningful cosmos. Without it, we begin to sound like Jean Paul Sartre: despairingly aware. Existentialism may not work for you but it is painfully rational.

Having overcome, by fiat, the most difficult question, a second question emerges on its heels: why did god create anything, including us (biological consuming – excreting tubes)? This is where the theologians get stuck. "Well, you see," you can hear them begin, "god was lonely…"

Stop it. How can perfection be flawed by something so human as loneliness? How can a perfect being interact with his own creation as if he were human? To be aware of oneself as alone and to know that creating self-aware biological units can cure it is divine madness. On the other hand, maybe god became bored again with the limited way it all worked out. It appears to be pretty much a one-way relationship. Apparently god spoke to us but that was a longtime ago. God doesn't seem very talkative anymore.

With god being so non-communicative, was the expectation that we would just wait around until the spirit moved god to speak to us again? He should have learned from the Hebrews. You remember the story. Moses went up on Sinai to speak with god and while he was gone, his people starting partying like there was no god and no tomorrow. All Moses did was turn his back. God should have learned from that.

Let us assess our condition: we are traveling through space on a ball of molten rock, ancient ice, sloshing water, and gases on an elliptical orbit of a rather small star, spinning dizzyingly on a shifting axis, where storms rage, tiny life forms, arguably intelligent, kill and eat one another.

There are known events in which humans have slaughtered millions of humans in outrageous frenzies of hatred. The horrors are so well known that the details are too numbing to be repeated often.

And they claim, these humans, to be created in the likeness of god. This is a god, therefore, that we may not wish to know too intimately. Why would god place his tiny, look-alike images in such dire straits? Is the motivation Self-hatred? Or do we represent a failed experiment that somehow got out of control and, ashamedly, he has turned his back?

Perhaps these conditions were created for us so that we may be humble and find something in that humility that will make us better. The question persists: better than what and on whose scale? Why didn't god create less stressful circumstances for his little supplicants?

Because we have busied ourselves with creating things, essentially useful to our survival, we have not spent much time asking the big questions. When one is hungry, cold, and struggling to create safe, nurturing spaces on this tumbling zoo, one is more likely to ask for survival guidance.

Wherever that guidance comes from is where we go again and again. It doesn't matter whether the guidance was merely a coincidence of the time the question was asked and the second event, which could have merely been a lunar eclipse. The lunar eclipse, occurring obviously during the day, answers the question because they are coincident. What is the answer? It will be read in whatever way the shaman sees it, whatever conceptual predeterminants were in play.

39.   Wednesday, November 2, 2005

BUSH ANNOUNCES $7.1 BILLION FLU PLAN

RUMSFELD STANDS TO PROFIT FROM FLU VACCINE SALES

CYCLING BY THE LA RIVER©

Fence sitting hawks, chocolate mares
Free men, stretched out with their drooling dogs
Near the fence, mattresses in the high grasses...

The bike path doglegs for five miles
Alongside the Los Angeles River...

A river with a cement bottom, its sloped and smooth
Graffiti speckled banks are exaggerated defenses
Against a tamed, muddy thing, with its heart swollen with trees askew
Bushes, wild grasses, birds, long legged strutters
Dipping their skinny beaks into the stream...

Speeding lines of young, smooth faced men,
Snug in colorful kits and sleek impenetrable glasses
Bent over their machines while grasping taped bars
Urging every erg of power out of their shaven legs...

Families on wheels meander, the youngest,
Distractedly drifts across the line, gazes up in amazement,
Smiles, and drifts back to safety
The eldest eyes my machine like a merchant, crisp in blackness
Lean and sculpted from fine metal and carbon

And we are, as she said, stardust
We are million-year-old carbon, and we have to get ourselves
Back to the garden...

THE RELUCTANT JIHADIST

And the path, a crest then falls, traveling beneath the street,
Then bridges another, passes soccer fields, dog runs
Then inclines up to the ending gates, and then the park
With rolling hills, golf course, then picnic grounds and gentle climbs
Back around, yoked ponies dulled for the children,
Miniature trains for old men ambling in their lost childhoods,
Gentler climbs, and the golf course again...

I dive down the long slope
Raising the gear to just beneath pain,
I've slid up on the saddle, riding close to the nail
To move my knees forward above the pedals
And, finally, embrace the pain...

That waits for me on the following hill
Then the path flattens and moves me down
To the burial ground, until I rise up to a television land
Before circling and descending to the path alongside the river.

40. Friday, January 13, 2006

HAJJ STAMPEDE KILLS AT LEAST 345 MUSLIM PILGRIMS

BAKKAH©

I was there
That place of rocks and visions
Where sparkling bodies buzzed
Above twitching goat ears
Dung steaming in the dust

That place of tears and austerities
Desolate and seductive
Crowded in my mind as the blanched sky bled
Dryly over unbroken ground and bleached stones boiled hot
As desert ghosts

I saw the black stone
Through American eyes
And moved among the circumambulants
We were dancers from a thousand lands

We were there
Sustained by a million beliefs
Honed to a fine oneness

When rain fell oblately;
When the tents and the tenants burned as we watched
Through tears
Cries rising in columns of smoke
Gas canisters exploding
Thunder stunning our hearts
We were breathless and afraid

We were diminished as our shadows fell
Covering the spaces once warmed by the sun
As realized then on our arms and faces
While the night crept again toward us.

THE RELUCTANT JIHADIST

41. Wednesday, January 18, 2006

IVORIAN YOUTHS BLOCK STREETS

THE MULBERRY BLUES°

Dark hued women filled gourds of Las Moras' cool waters
That also nourished her mulberry shrubs
Laden with sweet black fruit
Illustrative of the melancholy of a blues people:

Stolen from towns and villages
Bartered for guns and jewelry
Captured in battles; suffered brutish
Middle Passage travails

Chained to creaking slavers dressed to the nines
Forsaken along the path of hurricanes
Walked the trail of the Great Unspeakable
Littered with unmarked graves as milestones

Living between alien mythologies
Posturing as sacred truths
Down to the borderland where nobody knew their names
They knew to flatten the third and the seventh
When their voices rose with work or prayer.
They were old African souls in new world skins
Their mellifluous tongues alive as endured rainbows
Bluesy as ripe mulberries

The Southerners warned their children of this evident
Conundrum when they christened the springs Las Moras:
Sweet mulberries or Moorish women,
They left its precarious meaning to ruminations:
Moors and mulberries, feared and mythic, false
Polarities confounded to perplexing thoughts.
Their realities dangerously inseparable.

Mascogos laid claim to Las Moras' mulberry shrubs
Where the drift of night-borne air
Became a cooling spectral congregation
That hid from the noontime burn and provided
Comfort evocative of low slung
Black tents clustered in the Sahara

They wanted to farm the hard land
Graze herds and flocks, marry daughters to cousins at
Dos Nascimientos Across the Rio Bravo.

They desired welcoming songs
Prayers to god, now dressed differently
Yet still reliably there
When all else failed, they recalled the old ways

This is a hymn of the Mascogos
For those who have died, whom we shall not forget
Nor the global paths they traveled
Their blackness as sweet as ripened mulberries
That stained their still mellifluous tongues
Voices as deep as the traveling Africans
Still singing praise songs rooted in that which came
When the world was young
The Sahara was a land of rivers and trees.

42. Friday, January 27, 2006

CANCER PATIENT AND MEDICINAL MARIJUANA ADVOCATE DEPORTED FROM CANADA

THOSE BLUES IS OLD BLUES
The mulberry tree's relationship with the Blues is as ancient as the mythic love story of Pyramus and Thisbe. This story, in all its sadness, explains why mulberries are dark red.

Thisbe and Pyramus were young lovers who, although their parents' homes had a common wall, could not see each other because their parents opposed the idea of them having a relationship.

They would sometimes steal away and meet beneath a white mulberry tree near a river. One night when they were to meet, Thisbe arrived first and noted a lioness finishing a bloody meal near their rendezvous' tree. The lioness frightened Thisbe so that she ran away, dropping her cloak. The lioness mauled the cloak with her bloodied jaws and wandered away.

When Pyramus arrived, he found the bloodied cloak and imagined that Thisbe's had been devoured by a wild beast. In his agony, he committed suicide.

Sometime later, Thisbe returned and found her lover's body. She grieved as mightily as he had concluding with her own suicide but not without first imploring the gods to forever let the mulberry tree bear blood red fruit as a memorial to their great love.

That's ancient Blues.

These trees make decent wine, too. Although alcohol is a known depressant, when one has the Blues, wine can make everything a little more bearable, at least for a few hours. Lambert, Hendricks and Ross recorded a song with a hook that went, "Give me that wine, give me that wine! 'Cause I can't get well without muscatel. I ain't no use without my juice!). I rest my case.

Mulberry trees were also central to the production of silk.

Five thousand years ago, the Empress Xiling Shi picked a cocoon from a mulberry tree on the palace grounds. She accidentally dropped it into her freshly brewed cup of tea. She watched in amazement as a strong white thread unraveled before her eyes.

Mulberry trees proved an excellent home for silkworms. The trees were cultivated as hosts for silkworms as well as a source of a sweet, versatile drupe.

Although the Greeks or Phoenicians may have introduced the tree to Sicily, the Moors were the force that really cultivated it. During those times, the Moors turned Sicily into a major center of silk production. I could not resist trying to exploit the apparent relationship between Morus nigra and Moors. It felt so right but it is probably a coincidence.

Nevertheless, I feel certain that the apparent relationship between mulberries (moras) and Moorish women (moras) was not lost on the Spanish. It even brings to mind a rather mean rhyme we would recite as kids, "The blacker the cherry the sweeter the juice, you so black it ain't no use". Obviously, cherries do not grow on mulberry bushes but the equating of a sweet, black fruit with a person is the point.

My grandmother was raised near a creek named "Las Moras". She was born at Fort Clark Seminole Camp near the close of the 19th century. She would be described as a Black Indian or Seminole or Black Seminole or Mascogo.

There is the serendipity: we are an American Indian people descended from Africans who cultivated mulberry trees as the food source for silkworms (whose combined productivity made Sicily a silk production hot bed); Africans who were the victims of a genocide of such dimensions we have not seen since; Africans, fundamentally transformed but still recognizably African, who eventually arrived at Las Moras creek. The Moorish women or the mulberries; its all sweetness.

43. Tuesday, February 7, 2006

ALBERTO GONZALES DEFENDS WARRANTLESS WIRETAPPING

JIMMY CARTER: WARANTLESS SPYING IS "DISGRACEFUL AND ILLEGAL"

CARTOONED MUHAMMAD
Recently, an obscure Dutch newspaper held a contest in which cartoonists were to draw images of the Prophet Muhammad. The results were published and angry mobs have been wreaking havoc throughout the Muslim world.

This bumps solidly against the West's view of freedom of speech. Actually, when I was a student of the late professor Raji Isma'il al-Farouqi, he insisted that the primary struggle of Islam was to open all borders so that ideas and philosophies may compete openly and aggressively for hearts and minds. His position was based on Islamic law.

So, it is with irony that Muslims are challenging freedom of speech. And it is such an insane challenge. How can Muslims justify the killing of non-Muslims based on a cartoon? Even the cartoonist should not be targeted.

The Iranians have a long cultural history of drawing images of the Prophet Muhammad (well, his face is never shown) and Ali as well as others.

I saw the image and was a little offended but hardly enough to rampage. Perhaps, it is my Western orientation. I believe in freedom of speech. Applying standards to that speech should remain a private matter and no public official should be called upon to judge its appropriateness.

Maybe some Muslims were offended by the Arabic slogan on his turban as much as the fuse emanating from its top offended them.

The expression reads, "No god except Allah and Muhammad is the messenger of Allah."

This issue is a manifestation of the culture wars that has exploded on the planet. I'd like to blame this on George Bush but the fact is he is only guilty of stoking the flames. There has been a growing animosity between the least intellectually oriented people on both sides of the culture wars. You have the neo-cons wedded to the so-called religious right and, on the other side of the divide you have these Wahhabis (who actually are distorting the teachings of Imam abd al-Wahhab). How can we tolerate al-Qaa'ida and its cohort? It is a great mistake to grant them a pass on the basis of their claims.

Muhammad was neither warlike nor reckless in his use of force to protect the nascent Muslim community. At any rate, he cleaned up his neighborhood before venturing out into the rest of Arabia. He cleaned them up in regard to monotheism versus polytheism, not Islam versus Judaism. He even adopted Jewish law when there was no relevant law yet revealed as Qur'an. That demonstrates respect.

Islam will never succeed in the West under the terms that al-Qaa'ida demands and for this I am thankful. I believe I have the freedom to be wrong, to worship whomever I decide to and only if I decide to.

This is basic to a free society and I think a free society is worth dying for.

THE RELUCTANT JIHADIST

44. Friday, February 10, 2006

ISRAELI GOVT. BUILDING "TOLERANCE" MUSEUM OVER MUSLIM GRAVESITE

SHIN BET CHIEF: "I'M NOT SURE WE WON'T MISS SADDAM"

A HEARTFELT APOLOGY
The preceding blog ended with a flourish. I sang, "We are an American Indian people..." which is not true and not what I had intended to say. And if you read further you will note that it is in the context of being of African descent. At first, I erred in my logic by equating authenticity with nativity. African Americans, being created anew here in America, experiments in social engineering, had a new nativity.

What I meant to convey is that we, African Americans, are authentically American. America is the site of our second nativity in the sense that our genetic make up reflects a history that says irrefutably we were created in America through the extinction of cultural ties with Africa accompanied by the effects of the genocide of chattel slavery. We have genes that reflect the complexity of our ancestry. These circumstances make us uniquely American that is to say, truly American.

I realize that the indigenous people in the Americas are usually referred to as Native Americans. However, their identities are more complex than that socio-political utterance. There are indigenous people called Lakota, for example. The word is not an idle one and links them to a tradition that witnessed the beginning of time.

African Americans have not even a vague sense of what their "Lakota" sensibility would be. Our history begins with America. We embody Africans (Mainly West), Europeans (North, West, and East), First Nations (Mainly Southeastern), and many others in a manner uniquely American.

The slave experience recreated us. Although we may have had diverse beginnings, we were commonly defined as property. When my grandfather was Nigger, your grandfather was Master. Your grandfather may have been Scottish while mine may have been Hausa.

When I traveled to Africa, each time I felt a palpable connection to the people and the land. Do not mistake this for romanticism; it is not as if I imagined that I was walking among the rightful heirs of the kingdoms of Mali, Ghana; or the dynasties of Egypt, the drowned Nubian lands. Rather, I knew of the struggle to resolve the conundrum of colonialist mapmaking in Africa, of the denial of human rights in many countries. Yet I also understand that I was born and raised in the United States.

I connected with students at Khartoum University where I delivered a lecture and became engaged in discussions that allowed me to exploit my Arabic language skills.

Some of the music of the Sufi brotherhoods summon the Blues.

The same thing happened in Northern Nigeria. The people and I connected. One Thursday, I visited the Old Market in the city of Kano. The next day, I attended the Friday prayer at the central mosque. When I shopped, Friday afternoon and Saturday, the merchants, having recognized me at the Friday prayer, often refused to let me pay for the cloth, books, and other souvenirs I sought to purchase.

And there was the music that ranged from the Jackson Five to beautiful players who had no agents and no record label contracts. Same thing in Kenya. I found comfort in Africa's black and brownness; in its music that was already vibrating inside me; in the humor that sometimes surprised me in its innocence. Africa was very, very good to me.

And we, African Americans, with our uniquely American nativity, continue to contribute. And so it goes.

THE RELUCTANT JIHADIST

45.   Tuesday, February 14, 2006

DECADE-OLD CONGRESSIONAL MEASURE TO GIVE
ENERGY COMPANIES $7B WINDFALL

FOR HENRY LOUIS GATES AND THE GENETIC TRAIL
I belatedly watched the PBS special hosted by Dr. Gates in which they traced the biological origins of a panel of talented and interesting African Americans and himself (of course, he's accomplished and interesting, too).

The science was interesting and convincing, as DNA analysis has moved from science to truth. We believe in the results of DNA analysis. How could we not?

Among the nine participants, only two had Native American genes. Gates used this fact to debunk the histories many African Americans have inherited and created in which a significant ancestor was said to be Indian. Often, there were descriptions of ancestors that included the stereotypical features of Native Americans that happened, coincidentally, to be highly valued by those telling the stories: straight hair; narrow noses; lighter skin tones; exotica.

Some of us conclude that these stories are mythic because they are so profoundly informed by what are arguably signs of self-hate. The fact that the stories contain mainly descriptions of traits considered favorable because they are closer to the "universal standard" imposed by the oppressive culture of the masters is considered a prima facie indictment of the story and the storyteller.

But there is an important dimension that Professor Gates and his cohort did not consider with the same scientific awe. The most important dimension of someone's heritage may or may not be the genetic heritage. Culture determines our social interactions more than our DNA.

Some of my ancestors were Indian by culture and, I think although I cannot prove, by blood. The blood could explain some of our family's common physical traits but so could some European ancestors whom we must acknowledge as well.

By my generation, the influence was probably muted. Although I identify with my ancestors and their other descendants, I realize myself as an African American. The Mascogo/ Seminole dimension is real and contributive but there is no doubt in my mind of who I am.

I have a friend who believes the earth is our hell. If this is true, does that mean that those of us who are experiencing the best of this life are, therefore, devils of some rank or other? How can good people be so graciously rewarded in hell of all places? At first, this was a joke, sort of. But the fact that we do not struggle to right the wrongs we witness makes us complicit and maybe, just maybe, devilish.

46. Wednesday, February 15, 2006

3 KILLED IN PAKISTAN AS MUHAMMAD CARTOON PROTESTS CONTINUE

OUR SECRET GOVERNMENT
Our government maintains secrets. These secrets are associated generally with national security but we expect it to also provide some level of protection to industrial and trade secrets.

There should be limits to what information our government can collect. It is problematic for those who have been identified as dissidents or malcontents or people simply outside of the mainstream, to trust that this information will not be used against them.

The government feels it is required to spy on everyone so it may protect us. As an African American Muslim I am not predisposed to trust that our government will treat me and others like me (minority ethnicity and socio-religious background) fairly.

The looming war between civilizations is being brought nigh by the outrageously jingoistic actions of the Crawford City Jester AKA G Bush. He wants to be John Wayne but he is working like Barney Fife. He pretends to know what is best for us but it is he who has gotten us into a war with a run down nation, previously destroyed by that heartless and basically failed embargo.

The best thing that could happen, and it would restore some semblance of hope among us, is for Bush and Chaney to be impeached and convicted of high crimes and misdemeanors. We could install a caretaker government until the next elections.

We still have to face cleaning up the mess we allowed him to create in Iraq and Afghanistan.

Corruption and secrecy go hand in glove as that hand goes deeper and deeper into our pockets, robbing us blind and killing our children.

47. Tuesday, February 21, 2006

65 COAL MINERS TRAPPED IN MEXICAN MINE

FROM MALCOLM LITTLE TO MALCOLM X TO AL-HAJJ MALIK ASH-SHABAZZ

I had two heroes as a teenager, at least outside of sports, one was John Coltrane and the other was Malcolm X. These men were sides of the same coin. Both shattered barriers to understanding and opened vistas of freedom that we could actually see or hear while attending to their messages. Both were African American men who did not allow anyone to question their integrity or commitment to what they believed in.

Malcolm is the major influence in my adoption of Islam. To be certain, there were other men who influenced me but Malcolm's analysis and intensity drove me to consider what he had to say. Everything made sense to me.

I felt enabled by his stern refusal of everything except the truth. However, after committing to the Nation of Islam, I couldn't follow through because of two crucial facts. I read the Qur'an before going to visit Temple No. 1 in Detroit. When attending the temple, the leadership discouraged us from reading the Qur'an without supervision. This was a transparent attempt to direct our understanding by interpreting everything for the new member as if the book was too complex or difficult to understand. I nearly got my "X" but I couldn't swallow the stories of 24 black scientists creating the white man, nor the mother ship waiting to beam us up (resembling the Christian concept of the "Rapture").

After leaving the temple without further pursuit of membership, I began an intense period of study and reflection. Since I was decidedly unhappy with the religio-political positions of the NOI, and there did not seem to be much of a visible community of Muslims, I studied alone.

Eventually, Islam must be expressed in a social context. I had to find other Muslims to fully grasp its social imperatives. This is when

I discovered that my attempting to learn to recite my prayers in Arabic was tragically flawed. Not one Muslim could grasp what I was saying.

Eventually, I hooked up with Hajj Samson (RA) who began teaching me how to recite my prayers correctly and other important information on how Muslims worship and behave.

This led to the formal study of Arabic at the undergraduate and graduate levels.

But back to Malcolm. I sought political allegiances with other Muslims based on the fundamental radicalization that I had undergone listening to and reading Malcolm X. However, the people who became crucial to my intellectual development shifted to men like Hasan al-Banna, Sayyid Qutb, Mawdoudi, Tijani Abughideiri, Hasan al-Turabi, and others. You can see how radicalized I had become.

I dreamt of struggling to establish an Islamic state – somewhere. Here in the USA, I felt we should be able to establish majority Muslim communities in which some of the elements of Islamic law could be practiced. I thought these practices must be open and legal and not threaten anyone with the prospect of being disadvantaged because they were not Muslim. Rather, these communities could reflect the golden age of Islam that was experienced in Andalusia, not Arabia.

It was hard letting these thoughts wither as I reverted to my aloneness, rejecting the compromises that remain on the table because no one even cares enough to clear it.

48. Thursday, February 23, 2006

NIGER DELTA MOVEMENT KIDNAPS
OIL WORKERS FOLLOWING BOMBING RAIDS

DISAPPOINTMENTS: MUSLIMS AND FIRSTS NATIONS
Disappointing Muslims
When the fateful cartoons were spread throughout the Muslim world, Muslims did everything they could to make themselves look ridiculous. They fell into a neat trap that will take years for them to extricate themselves.

Imagine a neighbor posting pictures of your family that are clearly caricatures and designed to insult. Your family, in response, angrily beats each other, causing certain death to some of the weaker kin as a means of protest.

The message to their enemies is clear. When you want a few Muslims to die, say something bad about Islam and they will get so angry that they'll kill themselves. "Where can I sign up for this religion?" I can hear the people shouting.

It may be related to the oversimplification of the international struggles they face that creates this sense of rebellion. As Camus pointed out in his classic, "The Rebel", the first step toward revolution is rebellion but rebellion is not revolution. Rebellion is a striking out at symbols or anyone near or in the way. It suggests riots more than guerilla wars, violent and petty criminal behaviors rather than organized crime. The rebel may have a sense of the source of angst. In those lucid moments, the rebel may begin to consider the costs and benefits of revolution. At this juncture, the rebel decides. And the spectrum is wide enough to accommodate even the fanciful.

The rebel can become a revolutionary with the creed: by any means necessary. The rebel can be overwhelmed by the weight and density of the problem and become more accommodating to the governmental intrusions for the sake of getting along. As I've noted, the spectrum is wide and these are just two places where your token may land.

The question is whether this represents a pre-revolutionary phase or simply an orgasm of violence to release the growing tensions in the area.

I think the latter. There will be revolutions in the Middle East but the constituents will not be liberal democrats. Rather, the factions that emerge will be ethnic and religious. There has been a storm brewing in the ME for decades. Its forces are Shi'a and Sunni. The Shi'a are concentrated in Iran, parts of Iraq and parts of Saudi Arabia.

When the war in Iraq ends (the civil war, not Bush's war - that's a preliminary although initiating event), there will be three nations: Kurdistan, and two so far unnamed other sectarian states.

Disappointing First Nations People
When the First Nations people were under siege by the expanding European colonization, African Americans often joined their ranks and in some complex ways. Sometimes, AA's became actual members of the tribe and mixed genes (not really that frequently); other times AA's were held nominally as slaves although they were essentially free (Seminoles are an example); and at other times they were held as chattel slaves and treated poorly (there are reports like this from the Cherokees).

This complexity confuses attempts to assess the relationship among First Nations people and those of African descent. We have romanticized the relationship because it felt good to have a companion in our racial gulag. It also gave us a sense of connection to a sanitized past.

For some of the current issues between First Nations and AA's concerning gaming revenues, we should embrace the truth of our past as well as the irony of our present.

One of the ironies is that First Nation's are using DNA testing to determine who is a tribal member. They are using the technology of their conquerors and oppressors to oppress others. At the time the treaties were written, tribal membership was not necessarily by establishing a genetic link. There were generally several ways to become a part of a tribe.

Nevertheless, African Americans should let it go. It seems we go from one people's table to another's. If we had a stronger identity based on the realities of our circumstances (in other words, authentic), we could draw from all of our historical experiences, and forge ahead.

The conundrum for us is that we are a people forged in another's imagination. Malcolm X once said, "Where is Negroland?" confronting the mythic origins of African Americans.

Instead of channeling our energies in a manner that either confronts our society's inherent contradictions expressed as racism like Martin King did or we look more inward for a social change like Malcolm did, we have to do something other than stand in the shadows hands outstretched.

Either we are "Stand around the Fort" African Indians or "Handkerchief heads" African Americans.

We should be exactly what our history and our will dictate. The fact that we are associated with Africans, First Nations, and Europeans is simply fact. Whether the genetic "proof" of these historical relations is available is only interesting, not factually relevant. The culture from which we have emerged is rich with complexity and mystery. There is enough to give us creative license with our designation of new goals.

What do we want to be when we mature?

49. Monday, March 6, 2006

UN WARNS OF MASSIVE FOOD CRISIS IN KENYA

BOCA RATON IN THE HOUSE
I have one brother and two sisters. We are pretty close in age, especially the three older. We had parents that provided us stable homes, a consistently healthy diet, private educations, and primary medical care from the same providers for many years. They introduced us to music, the arts, literature, and sports.

Our parents honored us by acting out their love for their children. They prepared us to have fulfilling lives, whatever the odds.

Two of us live in Southern California. One of us has a home in Michigan and a home in Florida. And the other lives in Michigan exclusively. Two of us have lived in California for many years. The point I want to make is that we are probably typical of a certain group of African Americans who, standing on the knowing shoulders of parents and grandparents, have achieved financial successes that places them squarely in the middle class.

We could have drifted apart, becoming more absorbed in our nuclear families, careers, and other diversions.

My father let me know that he wished us to stay close. My mother was equally emphatic.

At our father's funeral, we made a pact to get together at least once a year to celebrate our family. This was the first year and I think it was very successful. Next year we may take a cruise. We've spoken of Europe and Africa.

We are family and we don't even have to shout it; we're content to be it.

50. Tuesday, February 28, 2006

BOLTON: UN PLAGUED BY "BAD ANAGEMENT, SEX, AND CORRUPTION"

LAISSEZ LES BONS TEMPS ROULER!
Well, it is Fat Tuesday again. This, you must admit, is a quaint holiday. It is a day on which we are to express wantonly our corporeal desires as preparation for a period of denial. Think of it this way, since we know that for the next forty days we are going to do without something that we really, really like, in preparation we must experience every carnal pleasure imaginable. If I were your god, I'd be a bit disappointed.

Mardi Gras has a history that actually connects it to Rome's most ancient holiday. The Lupercalia celebrated the she-wolf's nursing of Romulus and Remus. Scholars are uncertain what god may have been the original inspiration for this holiday but it was certainly old and very popular. Apparently, Lupercalia was pretty wild but there does not appear to be a direct relationship between Lupercalia and Mardi Gras. However, Lupercalia and Mardi Gras both occur in the month of February. This month is named for the concept of purifying through heat (think "fever") and Mardi Gras precedes the 40 days of purification through fasting.

The Muslims celebrate Ramadan as the month of their fasts. Ramadan is taken from the verb RaMaDa that means to burn. Muslims historically relate the name of the month and the purification from fasting.

When you're letting the good times roll, don't pretend to be this religious person who believes so deeply in this or that and accept that you are here to party until someone tells you that its time to go home and get straight with your god. That's how you're playing it now; waiting until you think the inevitability of death is staring you in the face. Then you plan to straighten things out.

I've never been to Mardi Gras. I'd go but it seems a little over the top for my taste. Don't misunderstand. I like a good party but what is reported in the news about that old, rotting city perched on wetlands during Mardi Gras is more than I want to deal with.

51. Tuesday, March 7, 2006

BOLTON INVOKES MILITARY OPTION IN IRAN NUCLEAR WARNING

A DIFFERENT TAKE ON REVELATION
The followers of the Abrahamic faiths accept as fundamental the theological analogy that god is to man as master is to slave. I have accepted this analogy from the beginning of my intellectualizing what ultimately must be considered only a condition of my birth: monotheism expressed as Christianity and later Islamic. Whatever the specific vehicle, unrelated to the fact that these faiths are within the same general framework, the fact is that they present a very powerful deity who is more than willing to make us suffer for our slightest disobedience.

Why would god create humans? The answer has always been illusive. God seems pretty unhappy with us and punishes us regularly as we continue to get it wrong. But we are god's handiwork.

The Muslims speculate that god created humanity because god was a hidden treasure that desired to be known. Such a sweet sentiment until one realizes that in order for humanity to know god each of them would have to endure suffering and pain. And that pain might exist even after death if we go against god's will even though we never even asked to be here. On its face, it does seem arbitrary and cruel, doesn't it?

And the poor, poor prophets. Here we have good people, trying to do the right thing. Along comes god, picks them because they are good and forces them to accept the impossibly dangerous task of bringing god's message to humanity. The prophets are forced to bear this message. Does this suggest to anyone other than me that god has a communication problem? God could create us but god can't speak to us?

The forced nature of messengership reminds us that we are dealing with a god whose judgment and power is unparalleled yet god makes us suffer.

Modern Abrahamic monotheists propose that we have a loving god who wants only the best for us, like a doting parent. Yet they fail to address god's capriciousness; how god threatens even those who do not know the proper demeanor for a slave.

Within the Islamic tradition, god even calls us "slaves". If we acknowledge god's omnipotence, why isn't that enough? Why can't god show us some love then?

Does it not seem incongruent? An all-powerful god, threatening and punishing when it seems fairer and more in keeping with the lessons supposedly contained in the holy books, that god loves us, raise us as we strive to attain knowledge of god and the worlds god created.

This is not a throwaway thought, really. A god of love and mercy does not, first of all, have to prove mightiness. Love works.

Could the threatened demonstrations of power and might be reflective of the fact that bad things happen in the world to people and god is not there, apparently, to protect us from these awful events? Since god doesn't prevent them or prepare us for these events, we must rationalize why. The most convenient thing to do is to look inward for the clues. We must be bad, right?

Wrong. This behavioral model is all wrong. The paradigm doesn't work. We live in a world in which things sometimes just seem to happen. There doesn't appear to be a cause and effect in regard to our behavior; stuff happens and if you're too close, it'll happen to you.

The question lingers why would an all-knowing god punish creation for doing wrong instead of instructing and guiding it to the right.

52.   Tuesday, March 14, 2006

U.S. ARRESTS VIETNAM WAR RESISTER

LET THE MADNESS BEGIN!
The NCAA Men's Basketball Tournament is the premiere sporting event in the United States. There was a time of imagined innocence associated with college sports but we have all grown to realize that corruption accompanies money like fleas accompany dogs; and there is big money associated with college sports.

To the extent that the criminals do not influence the results of the games, I don't mind. I know that money has influenced basketball games in the past, as there have been enough scandals to prove the point. But I am naive enough to believe that criminals do not influence the outcomes. Only part of this is naiveté, as I also believe that the best criminals know how to make money regardless of the actual outcomes of games.

But this is about basketball. This is about some young man stepping into history as the new rising star. He will be compared to some hall-of-fame player. He will make the professional leagues but become a journeyman which is still pretty good money and if it is managed well, enough to make entire lives more comfortable.

Then there is the player who sees a few minutes a game; doesn't get drafted; fails to graduate; and ends up traveling to Italy where he fails to make the transition and comes home broke, jobless, and maybe angry.

Then there is the coach of the underdog who loves his boys for having shown so much character all year, and who quits and goes to a more established program based on the underdog's success. Now they're just a resume item.

Then there is the kid who brought the team's jersey because it looked so cool. And it was cool. Until he was shot because it was the wrong color or he refused to give it up or it made him look like that other dude who they had been looking for.

Then there is me: imagining being able to rise 46 inches to snatch that rebound and get the ball to the point guard flying up the left wing before I hit the ground... And I get it done! Then there is the memory of actually competing on that level in another sport. Then I remember how unprepared I was emotionally to take advantage of those opportunities and how I was walking the walk of a man in a boy's shoes. I don't know in retrospect whether those circumstances prevented me from committing more fully to the sport or if I was simply tired of football.

Then I see some young guy handle it all, the game first and foremost, then the interviews, the stupid questions, all of that. I admire how so many of these young men speak intelligently at such tender ages. I was never in a situation in which I had to perform as they do so I don't really know whether I would have risen to the occasion.

THE RELUCTANT JIHADIST

53. Friday, March 17, 2006

STUDENT DEMONSTRATIONS GROW
TO OVER 260,000 IN FRANCE

WAS IT A BANG? SO, WHO BANGED WHAT?
"A NASA probe found evidence of how the universe began. From microwave residue, investigators conclude that 13.7 billion years ago, the universe "grew from sub-microscopic to astronomical size" in "much less than a trillionth of a second." The good news: This confirms "inflation" theory, which says the sudden growth was caused by inflation. The bad news: Scientists "still have no idea what caused inflation." Cynical view: We already have a theory of creation with no causal mechanism. It's called religion." Excerpted from Slate.com 3-17-2006

Funny, isn't it? So, as I understand it, a very, very long time ago some "thing" exploded becoming the universe. This sounds like what I read in the Qur'an, excuse me. It says, and I translate, "Allah said, 'Be!' and it is!" Just like that. Now, the whole thing about evolution started later, after this event.

That is why some older creationists felt that the god set creation in motion like a watchmaker. Whereas, the analogy may seem quaint, it was appropriate for its time. As you should know, at one point watch making represented one of the highest forms of craftsmanship. Today, these watchmakers have all but disappeared as technology has led to more accurate and less expensive timepieces.

Questions that arise in my mind include whether our universe and the ten others proposed by M theory (and before that heavy gravity and most string theories as well) were created simultaneously. Since they are proposed to be parallel, one would think so which makes the creative moment even more remarkable. The question, however, might then be whether we are able to observe the creation of these parallel universes or theoretically, which is to say mathematically, demonstrate their existences.

If Allah is behind the creative moment, and, if truly omnipotent, is this the same divinity that is concerned with whether we obey certain dietary laws? From the grandest creative act we may know to trifling detail of our daily doings, Allah's knowledge is incomprehensible.

If Allah has set the evolutionary urges in motion at the time of the creative moment, why does Allah later interfere with humanity by sending conscripted messengers to plead with us to return to a path that we should be naturally inclined to accept and follow?

The paradigm we are forced to embrace if we are to remain affiliated with the Abrahamic faiths, is a spiritual alienation from Allah due to choices our ancestors made. After all, we are born in a state of forgetfulness. We have to be lured back to the truth because of our ancestors' bad behavior.

If Allah is all-powerful, why do we have to struggle against Allah's faux enemies? They have no chance of success anyway. Why can't we ignore these faux ones and get on with discovering more of our relationship with the real One?

Finally, we have to admit that if the Big Inflation is how it really got started, and there are probably other universes clustered out there somewhere, how do we derive our notions of specialness? Why do we think we are so important, cosmologically speaking? We seem to be inconsequentially tiny but obsessed with our own image to the point where we say that god looks just like us.

We made all of this stuff up, didn't we? as we faced the overwhelmingly perplexing universe(s). Maybe the seed to create this stuff was contained within the "thing" that expanded into our universe(s) in that trillionth of a second.

54. Monday, March 27, 2006

BARBARA BUSH DIRECTED
KATRINA DONATION TO SON'S COMPANY

DEATH TO APOSTATES?
There is this poor man in Afghanistan who found his way from there to Germany and back home again. However, when he returned home, he did so as a Christian. For the unenlightened, according to some Muslims, apostates are to be killed. The history of this position is long but not complex, especially for the Muslim who places the Qur'an as the highest standard and not as a parallel source with the Sunna. For the Qur'an is quite clear: there is no compulsion in religion.

For the budding Islamic scholar of jurisprudence, there are no abrogating verses and in this case, the Prophetic Sunna does not provide any contrary examples.

Abu Bakr, the first Khalifa, led the nascent Muslim community through a period of near disintegration following the death of its messenger-prophet. He was the commander-in-chief in the wars fought against those who decided against recognizing his leadership of the Muslim community. Sadly, the victims of the wars included many Muslims, Sunni and Shi'a as well as others who, today, would be called simply collateral damage.

These wars were conducted after the death of the messenger-prophet. Whether he would have waged war against apostasy seems to be addressed in the adage that his character was the Qur'an. That being the case, he would have recited the Qur'an and the matter would have been settled.

From the perspective of Abu Bakr and those companions who supported the decision that he be the Khalifa, the integrity of the community was threatened not simply from the point of view of losing resources (people, trade routes, natural resources, etc.). Rather, the very existence of the community was being challenged.

He felt he must forcibly remove the rebellious elements as the Muslim Umma transitioned into a new steady state, with secession in place formally. This also marked the institutionalization of the rift between the descendants of Ali and those who favored more participatory governance.

Had it not been for the Ridda Wars, apostasy would not have risen to the level of treason. Government always becomes the first among us. We surrender some of our rights to the government for the sake of lawful order and peace. As long as we do not act against the state in its most fundamental definition, we do not enter the realm of treason.

Would have the nascent Muslim community classed apostasy as a capital crime had those renegades rejected him and Islam peacefully?

None can answer this question, of course, but I raise it to make the point that law evolves in the context of the challenges faced by a community. As we have seen in our own time and in our own country, leaders resort to extreme actions to gain and to stay in power.

At any rate, Abdur Rahman should not be prosecuted, threatened, vilified, castigated, or even noticed for his act of faith.

Questioning his sanity, brought to mind the stories of Soviet hospitalizations as mental patients of those who challenged the state. This makes perfect sense. If you disagree with the state, you must be either a revolutionary or insane.

Summarily, there is no compulsion in religion. If you, as a Muslim, want to leave the discipline, whether you "become" something else is not the real issue, you should be able to leave without any discussion.

55. Thursday, March 30, 2006

ABRAMOFF SENTENCED TO 70-MONTH PRISON TERM

AMERICA'S FELONS PICK YOUR FOOD!
Thousands of high school students across the nation are leaving their campuses, marching in protest to the US Congress' plan to pass immigration legislation that will, among other draconian measures, make all undocumented alien residents felons.

The immigration of undocumented workers – and we should not forget the primary definition when describing this phenomena: workers – is a boon to the US economy and a source of worry for anxious America. Mexicans and other Central and South Americans immigrate to the US because the job market beckons. They do not come to this country to eat up our precious welfare, overthrow the government, convert everyone Catholicism, or any other fear that one may entertain.

EMPLOYERS OF UNDOCUMENTED WORKERS
ARE MISUNDERSTOOD
Of course, if there were no job market, there'd be no undocumented workers breaching the borders. Those businesses and individuals (think of when you hired that Latina as a nanny – we never seem to call Latinas "au pair"; just "nanny") are simply trying to make a buck and they're hiring whomever they can so they can provide the goods and services and at prices that are good for everyone except the felonious undocumented worker.

Just as America fails to address the demand side of the economic equation in drug trafficking, it also fails to address the demand side of the equation when it comes to labor distribution.

If America were to lock up the CEO's of those companies most egregiously violating the immigration laws, the others would fall into line and adjust their production costs accordingly.

Did I say adjust their cost? Certainly did. Products and services will definitely increase in cost. The fact is, the Congress knows this and will not act to deflect the attention from those sitting targets (the businesses) while chasing the illusive undocumented workers.

CONGRATULATIONS TO THE STUDENTS
It was important for the students to protest the likely criminalization of their persons and, to a lesser degree, themselves. This was an excellent opportunity for them to learn, first hand, civics, political organizing, values clarification, etc.

One teacher really disappointed me by castigating the students for their actions on the premise that they needed to be in school. My retort was that teachers needed to follow the students and teach from where they are going. Protect them from heavy-handed administrators who are more concerned about obedience than they are learning.

THE RELUCTANT JIHADIST

56.   Friday, April 7, 2006

SEN. HARKIN URGES DEMOCRATS
TO BACK CENSURE OF BUSH

A LITTLE CHANGE OF PACE
I'm sharing with you a poem I finished last night. Enjoy

MY BEST INTENTIONS°

Billion-year-old carbon, recently renovated
I dreamt I was African, Blood; I even had an original name
I mean, I was resurrected ancient black gentility
We mastered the stars when
Abraham was a twinkle in his daddy's eye

Our faces reflect the vastness of space: Blackness
Impenetrable mysteries where galaxies are born
Scaffolds for the planets, the seven heavens

When, later, I tasted the Saharan sands, I knew
The way to Timbuktu
Less than half-a-day away
Far from the shade of the Ka'aba
I was dropping the five everyday

Gathered as three on the road. Between the drops
We walked on, paced by a capella chants
Over the muffled rhythm of loping dromedaries
I could hear the songs of the sons
Wafting in the breeze, coming to us lessons from the past

I dreamt I was an African, Brother
Planning Hat-kaptah way down in Memphis
Where the Blues were first applied

I dreamt I was Mascogo, Blood, feathers and drums
White soldiers in the woodpile. Genetic
Confluences refract colors on our faces

Old souls, new skins

To save something of from where we came
When our backs were first to the sun
Our griots sang the blues, inoculating
African souls, at the subatomic level, thorough
Aural memories of Sweet Home
Can make us dance loose

Westward ho
We liberated our imported capitalized
Asses. We chose to run and then the gun
Mexico's mercenaries to US Scouts
Creating New World definitions
That allow me to speak with you today
This is not how I had it planned, Black
My dreams wobbly
On shaking scaffolds, whether for hanging
Strange fruit or warehousing deferred dreams
I intended better things

Sort of. When thirsty, do you contemplate the mysteries
Beyond the first swallow? True
Rebel hearts swell from a rage of brutal simplifications
Contemplation mystifies the process, change promises
No comfort; change and progress never married

This carbon bounces with Snoop-like tightness, Rakim responding to densities,
Alliterative extrapolations
All blossoms in blues, I said I dreamt
Oneness right here
Resolution in the blues

I dreamt I was African because I am
American rooted in the dense mud of the Nile
Ghanaian gold swelling my pockets, watermelons
Plumping in my sun
Blossoming in the shade of skyscrapers and barrios.

57. Thursday, April 20, 2006

YAHOO ACCUSED OF AIDING CONVICTION OF CHINESE PRO-DEMOCRACY ACTIVIST

FAMILY SIZED LOVE
I am third born in a brood of four. Our parents were hardworking, intelligent, fun-loving people from great families. It makes poor drama but great living having parents who are supportive and generally just solid folk. This poem reflects on that and more. Sometimes, I am more able to communicate in poetry, I think, than prosaically but everything has a place.

It was last Christmas, when I crash°
Landed at DTX, bright knuckled from the Midwest
Until touchdown because of exploding and turbulent
Skies –
At least, that how I thought it would be
But the skies were quietly weeping and cold to the touch
Which made me even happier
To rest my eyes on Anitta:
My soul's shelter in any storm.
She sometimes might leak, as older shelters are wont to do,
But she's home
Wherever I go to find her
When I find her
I find home.

This was the happiest sad Christmas a Muslim can have
As we so recently buried our Dad
And others, too, not long gone, haunt us, like the moon
Follows us as we turn and ride away

Embracing my brother, hugging a soldier, then a renegade,
Kissing the tender offshoots of our clan who have grown stronger, funnier,

And when you look into their eyes you can see the soul
Who was there before, wearing and slightly differing form

Gayle completes the set, and the promises we've all made
Are well kept, and we are stronger, somehow, because of our loses
Shared in moving rituals and mournful salutations
And the laughter that shakes us, all four,

When we remember
Under the influence
Which may be the only decent time
To step to those moments unabashed, unafraid of offense
Because when we awaken, we are
Sober and, therefore, disarmed of the passion, as a dissipating storm
Loses its eye, deterred from the mission that was once so clear.

At least I don't remember because tequila
Has burnt a hole in my memory. There are smoke filled rooms
In the back of my memory, tar soaked synapses slowly misfiring.

58. Monday, April 24, 2006

RUMSFELD OKS EXPANSION
OF SPECIAL OPS FORCES ACROSS GLOBE

LETTING GO... ANGER AND RESENTMENT COSTS SKYROCKET.
I awoke one morning estranged from a significant dimension of my emotional baggage. I don't really know how it happened. And it wasn't as if I had launched a prayer recently pleading for relief from my bondage to things past.

I rolled over and looked at my mate and realized that although I had not forgotten my beefs, they no longer had any real meaning.

Partly, it is related to finally forgiving myself for being less than I had hoped I would be. I wanted to be a better person than my life demonstrates I was. I had to acknowledge that failure. Having done that, it was easy to move to the next step to be the man I want to be.

This also changed my sensibilities about the divine.

It's all related.

Watch.

If I am no longer burdened by feelings of guilt and resentment, my relationship with the divine is not one of guilty supplicant but one of puny defiance manifested in my acting in ways that I judge as moral whether it is in a certain book or something that makes moral sense to me.

I still can remember all the bad stuff. Its not like I had a lobotomy. But the bad stuff seems a little hazier than before.

59.   Thursday, April 27, 2006

SNOW: BLACK UNDERCLASS
IS "MOST DANGEROUS THING IN OUR LIFETIME"

THE GOOD SON
I have a twenty-one year old son who is about to graduate from an outstanding university. No. It is not the University of Michigan. It is a pretty good school with a Michigan-like tradition of excellence. Some call it the Farm. Some just say its name: Stanford. Like Harvard. Two syllables. But to get all of the greatness of Michigan in two syllables is like forcing ten pounds of gold into a five-pound bag.

Anyway, my son has always been determined. Once he developed a sense of self, he has been unstoppable. I remember when he was learning to inline skate. We were on the bike path that meanders along Venice and Santa Monica Beaches. Like his father, he is not gifted with great coordination although, like his father, he is a better than average athlete.

He would fall repeatedly while attempting to master the two basic maneuvers required for success: stopping and starting, and it that order. Before you learn to start, it is safer to learn how to stop first. But, like the Adidas commercial with Dwayne Wade; fall down seven times, get up eight. And that is what my son did. Not only did he get up, he laughed at his own clumsiness. With that attitude, he became a good inline skater. Seeing this, I had confidence that he would be fine in this world.

Once I knew his character and disposition, I was certain that he would accomplish whatever he wanted. So far, I look like a sage.

He's going to take a year off from his formal education to work and relax a bit. I think he has earned a little rest and I am not concerned that this hiatus will have a negative impact on anything he decides to do later.

When he returns, he will attend medical school.

I was talking to a dock mate last weekend and we agreed that we should be a little reluctant to take credit for the success of others, even our own children. They do the work we just provide the opportunity. They make their own choices. By the same token, if my son had become a hoodlum, I would not want to be blamed for his poor decision. He would have made it, not me. And all of us know of families in which the children were provided with all the essentials including love and one or more of the children adopted criminal behaviors.

So, while I am proud of him for his accomplishments, I am really proud of his character. He is a good son. Although I wish he would call me on the telephone more often.

60. Tuesday, May 2, 2006

FLORIDA LAWMAKERS MOVE TO HELP FELONS REGAIN RIGHT TO VOTE

THE RIDDLE OF PERPETUAL ANGER
I'm certain that you recall the comedic stylizations of Rodney King's famous rhetorical question about "getting along". We may have been amazed, or, more likely, stunned by the simplistic innocence of that comment. Of course, you recall that King was the victim of wanton police violence.

A very brief recapitulation (why is That word so long?): he was speeding; police pulled him over and beat him while on camera like some TV reality show. He became the symbol of black and brown men being abused under the cover of law; in other words, the police had a right to stop him but they exceeded reasonableness the way they literally kicked his ass.

No one, to my knowledge, ever answered King's sincere question. Look at it this way. Let's say you were in a relationship for twelve years. The first third was miserable for whatever reasons. The second third was better but the scorecard was marked: improvement needed. The last third may have seen the subject raise his game. His mate, however, is still fuming because of the troubles associated with the first stage.

When they discuss their issues, her anger is visibly present. She acknowledges that his behavior has really improved. But her anger continues to burden the relationship unbearably because it poisons simple communication and castrates Cupid.

Does any of this sound familiar? We know anger is debilitating. We know that if you stay angry and non-communicative for extensive periods, the relationship is going to end. And so might you. We also know that this kind of stress kills. It sustains itself despite being so emotional and physical taxing, even if its cost is our lives.

If death doesn't get you to sit up straight, there are other drawbacks. Relationships have echoes. If you have long-term anger, your mate will sense the anger and lose interest. The relationship, anger at the helm, is headed toward D Day. Decision Day is the very day the decision to end the relationship is communicated. Unless you feel, D Day is your goal, you may want to consider shedding your anger or aiding your mate in that struggle.

61. Friday, May 5, 2006

FEMA TO CLOSE NEW ORLEANS RECOVERY OFFICE

THE PEOPLE OF ZUG
One of the most otherworldly places in Detroit is Zug Island, a man-made Island dedicated to the transformation ores into steel. This is a hellish process. It is dangerous to the workers and dangerous to the people who live near ground zero. The following piece is dedicated to the victims and their memory.

STEEL PEOPLE©

Zug Island,
Scowling god of steel,
Heart burning a constant 2000 degrees,

Blood running thick molten white, becoming
Trimmed blooms to rail ties, skyscrapers,
Prisons and bridges.

Delray cowed, indistinct in sulfuric clouds
Shrouded the modest houses, all grim lepers,
Their painted skins sloughing,

Dusty patches and bare summer trees,
Missing children, down in the yards
Rummaging boxcars.

At the red river's edge,
Their backs to the immutable world,
Fearing its gods,

Multicultural despair embraced dreams
In the clouds of Zug:
Hunkies. Gypsies. Hillbillies. Negroes

 Lighting candles in the dark
Churches, kneeling on threadbare rugs

THE RELUCTANT JIHADIST

Mumbling formulas of hope, casting spells.

Hardness sheds hard things;
Steel people, trimmed blooms,
Warehoused on the red river's bank.

62. Monday, May 8, 2006

REPORT: INTERNATIONAL AID WORKERS SEXUALLY EXPLOITING GIRLS IN LIBERIA

GOD, THE MISOGYNIST
The purpose of authority is to outgrow it. We have outgrown the authoritative nature of the Abrahamic faiths. Regardless of how gender friendly they may have been at their beginnings, they certainly are male centered today. This orientation forces us to face the dilemma of our changing perspectives on gender in our social milieu while our faith systems hold us to a standard of expired centuries.

The religions that glory as descendants from Abraham, in contrast to other religious traditions throughout the world, do not have any female symbolism for god. Although these religions propose their vision of god does not include a sexual dimension, they, each one, use masculine pronouns when describing the divine.

However, there are indications that many Christian Gnostics did use female symbols. For example, one group argued that if God created us in His image, his image must be masculo-feminine. Those who rejected this idea won the battle.

The most striking conversation was over the very nature of the divine. Some of the Gnostics felt that they were actually "children of the father, while the non-Gnostics were "children of the demiurge (a demiurge is a minor god thought to be the father's operative managing earth)".

However, within Islam it is a little different. Male pronouns are used throughout the Qur'an as referents to god. The best example is the chapter that answers the question, "Who is God?" It can be translated as, "Say, He, Allah is One. Allah is He on whom all depend. He begets not, nor is He begotten. There is none like Him." The question never arises, except for the careful reader.

There is a verse in the Qur'an that translates as, "He created the male and the female..." The expression is unusual in the Arabic as it uses a rare pronoun "Maa" which has no sexual dimension. The commonly used pronouns are either male or female; Arabic features only this rarely used neutral pronoun. In this instance it is clear that the message is that Allah does not have a sexual dimension. Of course, all modern theologians in the Abrahamic traditions will argue against associating any human descriptors with the divine.

Well, they started it. It is not enough to point out this one instance of non-male symbolism.

The mystics of Islam have described creation in terms of male and female energies. Allah has the creative capacity in "Dhaat". This is where all physical creation emerged and it is decidedly female. This may seem strange but when it is related to the two most common descriptors in the Qur'an in reference to Allah, it makes sense.

Every chapter in the Qur'an (except the 9th) begins, "In the name of Allah, the Compassionate the Merciful". The words, "compassion and merciful" derive from a common root (RHM). This root has the meaning of "womb". The Qur'an, therefore, uses female symbolism that is only available to those who read and understand Arabic. The problem is that many Muslim men read this and don't want to think about its implications.

If the Gnostics were right, and those who formalized the church with its male hierarchy are worshippers of the demiurge while they worship the father, then it would be fair to say that the Muslims are probably liturgically closer to the Gnostics but in practice, to the right of the modern Christian world. Muslims' abuse of women is legend. Their disenfranchisement was always contentious for us born and bred Americans. Exactly where we would be if not for strong men and women? Would we have survived the middle passage? Slavery? Steel plantations?

The thing is, none of the religions within the Abrahamic tradition honor women. It is as if these religions were cooked up in the hunters' lodges while the men waiting on the mastodons.

I can see them now. Gathered around the fire, waiting for ESPN. They begin to tell each stories of their dreams in which their fears abound. They use their dreams to explain the canopy of stars; the lush savannahs; the winged and fleet of hoof; and why they abjure the company of women.

THE RELUCTANT JIHADIST

63. Wednesday, May 10, 2006

UNCOVERED LETTER SAYS YALE SOCIETY
STOLE GERONIMO'S REMAINS

Universal Dream Machine

Now Hawking thinks the universe is a dream
Sparking synapses in the actuality of the divine
And that we cannot fathom divine dimensions
As we are palpably dreamt realities ourselves
Aswim in the mind of the divine

Can the dreamt apprehend the dreamer?

A dreamt world firing in the synapses
Of the non-existent, non-contingent
Undreamed, unknowable one –

To dream is to first sleep, becoming unaware
As the dreamer sleeps, we suffer unbeknownst to the dreamer

When the dreamer wakes and hears the cacophony of prayers,
Being dreams' memories, the dreamer weeps
As we drift into the remote network of synapses less fired
That region of lost, unremembered things

So we die in the divine's dreaming
As we die, we cascade as sparks falling
As falling stars
Disappear in the night
Into the emptiness that our prayers could not fill
Nor silence the sucking sounds around our heels –
Choked up, we smile our resignation
And fade, feet first, as in a cinematic transition
To black.

64.   Friday, May 12, 2006

BUSH'S APPROVAL RATING SINKS TO 29%

PHANTOMS AND DREAD
Phantoms to the right of us, phantoms to the left of us – how are we to manage?

To the right of us? Preemptive and redemptive wars are being waged for the liberation of long-suffering victims of non-Christian dictatorships. Never mind the irony that is our countrymen financing those dictatorships for the sake of economic security. If you read the previous sentence without cringing, then you are still confused as to what these wars are really about. It is not about national security; rather, it is about the security of international corporations' interests here and abroad.

How else would you expect them to behave? These phantoms? You elected them to office to do exactly what they've done. It is not enough that you were afraid. We have all known fear. It is that you voted for Bush and allowed him, through the courts, to garner the votes even of those who voted against him.

Big oil and Halliburton are natural allies. These men do not have to gather in smoke filled rooms to strategize. They have exactly the same interests and the same education and training that compound to create silent conspiracies derived from common interests.

The war of occupation in Iraq still has not succeeded in bringing to power those who may have or are likely to develop common interests with the USA. The Iraqi oil is still not secured. The country has been engaged in a low-grade civil war for months (unless you drank the Kool-Aid).

Phantoms to the right of us. The war on terror scares the literal shit out of me. After all, my name is Umar; I have traveled throughout the Middle East and Africa. The Bushies put whomever they want in jail; they torture and arrange for torture; and we allow it because we are afraid. Our fear is rational. Their struggle against our interests is rational. What is irrational is how we, them and us, choose our tools to work through these naturally conflicting interests.

When the president couches the struggle in religious terms, he is, in fact, reflecting some strong currents within this nation flowing toward some kind of declaration of religious preference.

Phantoms to the right of us. Iran wants to melt things down and blow things up. The very thought of it makes me cringe. Think of what the consequences might be: a power that throws its weight around, willy-nilly changing governments in the region to be more consistent with how they know god wants them to rule. Bush should let them know that there is room at Guantanamo Bay, and you don't need reservations.

Bush says, "Walk softly and carry a big stick. When you're close enough, hit'em with the stick as hard as you can!"

Phantoms to the left of us. Please, Mr. Bush, protect us from the terrorists within our midst. Have the NSA read my mail just in case I've decided (or one of my personalities) to join a terrorists cell to do some violence. Listen to my telephone calls just in case Osama calls me seeking donations. As for my e-mail, hey, it's out there, right? I am so afraid, just like you said, ever since Nine Eleven. I mean I need some heavy-duty protection. Who's that?

Phantoms to left of us. How high should the fence really be? Should it be a double fence? What about if we like, put some bamboo sticks in hidden pits? No, I'm not talking about Israel. No, I'm not talking about Mexico. I'm talking about Canada. Don't you remember that they actually caught a terrorists coming across the Canadian border intent on blowing up LAX? Let's build a couple of walls – Mexican and Canadian. Then those damn beaches! How are we going to keep the Islamo-Fascists from hitting the beaches? Then again, what if they're already here? Oh yeah, the telephone thing.

Phantoms to the left of us. Mr. Bush, please save us from gay marriage. Do you know how excited you sound when you're decrying gay sex? What are you thinking then? Just wondering. I know it's a little irritating to have to listen to people who think everyone cares about their sex life. But what can you do? We've got to listen until they get bored with boring us.

Phantoms to the left of us. Can a person truly be illegal? Can a person's existence be a violation of the law? Oh, Bob, sorry but, um, you're, like, unlawful so you've got to go to jail. Bob cannot be illegal. He can break the law but not by his very existence. His existence in a certain space could be illegal or unlawful unless he can demonstrate that he has permission to be there (like in your house, in the bank vault after dark, or, yes, even in the nation). Bob needs something authorizing him to be in the country, which is usually presented, in some kind of a formal document (birth certificate, naturalization papers, green card – which isn't really green at all – more gringo deceptions!).

I'd rather think of Bob as undocumented. Furthermore, we should all understand the hypocrisy of prosecuting Bob when the true criminals are those businesses that have let Bob and others know that once they trek across the border there is employment waiting. The hypocrites never acknowledge the market forces at work but on this one I have to give Bush a pass.

Phantoms. We dread disruptions to our routine comforts. This dread is the mother of all phantoms. We will authorize killing for oil as long as we're not asked in advance. We will build walls to keep Them out; and the them is not necessarily Spanish speaking. Our dreads will bury us.

65. Thursday, May 25, 2006

WEINER: UN PALESTINIANS "SHOULD START PACKING LITTLE PALESTINIAN TERRORIST BAGS"

Fire Fly©

Jar agape, top agrip
the stalking child shadows
a flying glitter of flaming beetles

While darkness swarmed
flooding the horizon, muffling
day noises, sparking
nocturnal lights of our refusal
to submit to the usual spin

Inside the tented blanket
the hunter-child, home now
held, topped jar
the solitaire firefly flashing
the bluest signs
that slow and dim
under fretful child eyes
swelling in wonder, tearing in awe
Aware
now a child's possessing
love's first lesson.

66. Friday, May 26, 2006

ACTIVISTS, CELEBS STAGE ENCAMPMENT FOR SOUTH CENTRAL FARM

After the Rain°

She left Saturday morning, when the rains eased
Clouds lumbered to the hills then rested, disrobing

The fully risen sun, straddling valleys to the east
Burnt lingering mists in the wood's canopy, disclosing

Winter ravaged landscapes, seen through retired raindrops
Glistening on the windshield, random glorioles

Beaded gems of refracted meditations, speaking
Her blues that would not yield to the storm's

Fresh residues in all spectra and forms
She, again, found that lost Thing

Strapped behind the wheel, gazing into the fresh glare
Spelled out in glittering rivulets, zigzagging

That Thing, her spectral mirage
Coaxing her to love's ultimate sabotage

His smile dissembled every feeling her leaving evoked; as if
He were somewhere else, watching someone else

Leave someone else, in the Saturday drizzles
After all, she was gone, really gone

THE RELUCTANT JIHADIST

We will Never Know°

We will never again know the sky
As we did when our bones were fresh

We see skyscrapers poking their metallic heads
Through a sallow haze girded by mountains

We will never again see clear to the moon
The fog formed at the convergence
Of passion and greed dims the vision

Subterranean sludge, viscous fluids underground
Movements piped below our pillowed beds
Beneath basement floors

To redemptive revivals conducted in huge
Baptismal pools. Chemicals. Heat Transubstantiation
Feces. Urine. Drugs. Untidy things

Homeless. Landfills have no land filling
Their swollen acres. They teem with what
We desire to forget. The broken

Mirror's bad luck; photographs of betrayers
Stolen children; misspent condoms
Undiscovered discarded babies

We will never again know the skies without
Purple and yellow striations
Encompassed fields of vision

An everlasting canopy of contrails
Adorns the ejaculatory spumes of wastes
Rising from plants
Garbage scowls wander the seas

Patriots without nations, explorers

Fingering their GPS's
Searching for a forgiving
Place that will embrace
Our cargoes of shame

67. Tuesday, May 30, 2006

INDONESIAN EARTHQUAKE DEATH TOLL TOPS 5,400

The following poem is based, in part, on a true incident; the "honey" is a fictional device used to make a point. A point, by the way, that is not fictitious.

The Two-Spoon Blues

My wife was gone
When the sun got bum-rushed
By the moon

I was almost alone
When the sun said don't come 'round
Here too soon

My new honey was 'bout to stir
Sugar in my tea
When the little girl called to me: Papi

She left rotten onions and just two spoons
Papi, two old spoons is loony tunes
So, I got the two-spoon loony tune blues
I got the two-spoon loony tune blues

But when my honey slowly stirs
The sugar in my tea
Her strirring is more than all right with me

Don't be too worried 'bout
My honey and me
We love to stir hot tea
And two spoons is all right with me

Just before the sun leaves the moon
Remind that old girl to not come
'round here too soon

68. Wednesday, May 31, 2006

UN SAYS AIDS EPIDEMIC IS BEGINNING TO SLOW DOWN

BABY KILLERS?
During the lifetime of the Prophet Muhammad and the lifetimes of the earliest to serve as heads of state after him, it was common practice to bivouac fighting soldiers outside of urban areas. It was understood by the commanders that mingling men who have been engaged in killing with a civilian population is a formula for disaster.

This is a lesson the US government needs to learn quickly. Today, soldiers killed two women and an unborn child. The driver was rushing them to the hospital where her husband awaited what should have been a joyous occasion. Only when they arrived he witnessed the doctors' failure to save the life of the baby. This reminds me of what sparked the 1963 Watts rebellion.

It is just wrong to have military killing machines serving as a domestic police force. And it is disingenuous to blame the Iraqi "government" for its failure to assert itself. Puppets don't know how to walk, let alone govern.

Do not take men and women you have trained to kill and ask them to police civilian populations; it is deadly unfair to the people and the soldiers.

New Orleans
It is hard for us to admit that the city is sinking fast. Satellite imagery has allowed scientist to measure the speed with which the area is sinking. It is apparently much faster than previously thought. They blame overdevelopment as well as excessive drainage of the water table (obviously associated with development).

Some of my people are from New Orleans. I've visited there several times. I know this is not politically correct to say but I never liked most of the city. It seemed old and poorly maintained. I've been in very old cities (London, Cairo, Kano, etc) but never have I seen a city that depressed me more than NO. Like everyone else, I love the food and music associated with it but the housing and commercial buildings in many areas of the city need to be razed.

Whether the development conspiracy theories are spot on, NO needs a well thought out development plan that it is not going to realize because it would require regional planning and this nation is weak on regional planning because of its unswerving commitment to private sector development. The problem is that sometimes profit and public interests are at loggerheads. The private sector always seems to win, especially the big wars.

Public Education
Here in Los Angeles, public education has become a more inflated football than ever before. Everyone is asking questions but I fear none of them are asking the right questions. They are asking: who should run the district? Should the district be broken up? How should public education be supported?

I'd like someone to ask: what will Jack, Jill, Jose, Maria, Muhammad, Aliya, Chan and Woo need to know to lead satisfying lives by contributing to the welfare of the many as well as themselves. How do we teach to discern good information from bad? What skills are predictably necessary? What are the most effective ways of learning?

Should every person in our society be bilingual? What is the appropriate level of mathematic skills?

Finally, how should we pay for public education?

69. Wednesday, June 7, 2006

LANDLESS WORKERS OCCUPY BRAZILIAN CONGRESS OVER LAND REFORM

AMERICAN EMPIRE ASCENDANT
Does the ascendancy of the American Empire disappoint you as much as it disappoints me? I would've hope for a benevolent empire in which its citizens and denizens would live in a world of peace and harmony. Okay. I was only joking.

Instead we have an empire that invades a state that it once collaborated with to destroy a neighboring state; threatens to bomb or invade a nation because the empire does not believe that the state wants nuclear energy for peaceful purposes. We have an empire like other empires.

Why wouldn't Iran want nuclear weapons? Think about it. Your neighbor was supported by the empire in a bloody war of attrition against you that harkened back to the tragic days of trench warfare. The war was conducted primarily because Iran is a Muslim state very desirous of being an Islamic state.

Now the empire occupies your old enemy's land. Now the empire threatens you with the complicity of its arch ally, Israel. Why wouldn't Iran want the bomb?

The thought that North Korea just might have a itty-bitty bomb, meant that the empire wanted to talk – a lot.

They would like to depict Iran as a rogue state but whom has Iran invaded? Wasn't Iran bombed by Israel, too? Don't you remember? It was about a nuclear plant that Iran was building and Israel thought not.

The American Empire is quick to kick ass. The problem is that it doesn't have the conviction to do anything but kick ass. It cannot sustain a campaign against a people with conviction, regardless of how wrong-headed it might be.

The push toward democracy theme in Iraq came to the game quite late. The goal was to defuse weapons of mass destruction. That point being mooted, the issue became the necessity of removing a vicious dictator. Can you imagine all of the dictatorships gasping in fear?

70. Monday, June 12, 2006

THREE GUANTANAMO DETAINEES COMMIT SUICIDE

FROM SWAGGER TO STAGGER:
THE CZECH DAGGER
The most storied event in the world of sports is underway. The FIFA World Cup is taking place in Germany this year. This is by far the biggest sporting competition in the world. When a nation wins this cup, they can rightfully claim being the best in the world.

To what extent does the teams' play represent their respective cultures? The Brazilians claim that the samba and their love of life are clearly represented in how they play, as they say, futebol. Rhythm, creativity, passion are claimed as defining characteristics by Brazilians. I don't know if this is true. I've only seen pictures of Brazil but what I have seen is complex but decidedly well in the flow of its mythic stature. You can see the passion, rhythm and creativity when Ronaldinho touches the ball. Then there's Robinho or Kaka running the front line with Roberto Carlos overlapping and bending the ball around the leaping wall into the upper left corner of the frame. This is, my friend, beauty.

Then you have the Germans. Stern but fragile in the back. Dull but relentless. The Czech Republic is big, battle-wearied souls unafraid and exploitive.

I haven't seen the Ghanaians but you just know they're going to dance even better than the Ivory Coast. Africa is the mother of rhythmz.

So now you probably have figured out what is lacking with the US of A. But let me be fair: the biggest problem is financial. The Americans do not pay soccer players well compared to American football, basketball, and baseball. Certainly American soccer players don't make anything near what players make in Europe.

The American players are drawn from the second athletic tier. Those on the first tier choose one of the American big three. Top tier athletes would also choose track and field over soccer because even amateurs fair better than soccer players.

The American team plays soccer with no rhythm, little passion, and less creativity. Bruce Arena is a good coach but he is very conservative. He started a 4 5 1 with the over-rated Landon Donovan as the withdrawn forward playing between the lone forward and the midfielders. The problem with this formation is that it bottles up the midfield. The Americans are smaller and less talented on the ball than their European counterparts. By clogging the midfield, the bigger stronger team is bound to dominate because speed and openness are compromised.

Bruce! Go to a 4 3 3. Bench Beasley. He is over-rated. Put Donovan as the center midfielder and give him attacking responsibilities. Put Eddie Johnson as the right forward. You've got to work the ball to him.

Landon Donovan disappeared in the game against the Czech Republic. Now we know why he wasn't interested in playing in Europe. His game isn't ready. The American press was saying ridiculous things like the team was walking with a swagger. It wasn't a swagger. The Czechs put a dagger in the swagger and now its all stagger.

The Americans best chance is against Italy. The Americans are going to swoon when the Ghanaians bring it. They will have passion, creativity and rhythm.

The Czechs have seen hard times in their country. Many of the players for the top teams come from difficult backgrounds. My impression of the American team is that many of them grew up in suburban America. One cannot dictate the circumstances of one's birth but it does inform how we are in the world.

Athletes born in the comfort of middle class America have not had the struggles that characterize the lives of most of the players competing in the World Cup.

I believe that urban poor kids will work harder than middle class suburban kids to earn a career as a professional athlete. I also believe that many of the European athletes worked harder than their colleagues on the American team because of similar circumstances.

The Americans will disappoint again on this big stage. I hope they emerge from their group but losing so badly to the Czech Republic while Italy looms ahead places them in the unenviable position of not making it out of their group.

71. Tuesday, June 13, 2006

FATAH SUPPORTERS STORM
HAMAS-CONTROLLED PARLIAMENT BUILDING

PEACE WHERE I LIVE
The brute in me recognizes the brute in you. I understand how you measure spaces in a room to determine whether you have enough pathways to safety. I've seen you walking in the neighborhood aware of all that is happening around you.

You learned that being indecisive can be fatal. You've made wrong decisions but for the right reasons. All of these psychological rationales echo in the emptiness of failure.

The brute in me says it is unlikely that we can ever tolerate failure. To tolerate failure is to deny that our aims are self-serving. Even when our aims are clothed in the sacredness of group interest, self-interest lies at the foundation.

The problem, then, might be in deciding what, in effect, constitutes a failure and this definition is likely to shift from problem/ opportunity to problem/ opportunity.

Take my wife, please.

We met. We fell in love. We planned to wed. We broke up. We got back together. We broke up. We got back together. We broke up. You're probably getting the picture. Then she asked me to marry her. I accepted.

She was living in Los Angeles and I was living in Las Vegas. Since I'm older and I am slowing down my professional career and preparing for another, post-retirement career, it seemed reasonable for me to return to Los Angeles so she could continue her career and begin graduate school.

So I took a job in Los Angeles earning quite a bit less than I earned in LV. I moved into a Northeast barrio known for violence against

African American men. I gave away, at her suggestion, most of my house wares.

The tragic back-story is that we were married but we were not intimate. In this usage, intimacy is not a euphemism for sex. I mean it in every respect.

How does one cope with these issues? My first response was to avoid them. Then I confronted them. I had to. The air had become poisonous. I explained to her that everyone needs a place that they can go to and be greeted in peace. We like to call this place home.

Her expressions of anger were strangely tied to events that had occurred long ago (we're talking years) and she misconstrued some of them. I was flabbergasted by her complaints. I think they were guises (a failed strategy, really) of searching for a reason to leave because of my relentless attempts to get her to address a few fundamental issues.

I'm shopping (Whole Foods & Trader Joe's), cooking, cleaning, writing (more!), and going out (well, eventually).

I do miss her but I also miss a toothache when it subsides.

I'm also shopping for home furnishings. I've new pots and pants, dishes, silverware, and a new television (World Cup!). I'm going to decorate with cushions and low tables for working, eating and relaxing.

I'm going to live on Wind Dancer on the weekends (at least during the summer and fall months). Life is good. All I need is a good woman. And they are very hard to find.

At least now there is peace where I live.

72. Wednesday, June 14, 2006

POLICE RAID CLOSES SOUTH CENTRAL FARM

POMP & CIRCUMSTANCE!
Tomorrow I leave Los Angeles to attend my son's graduation from Stanford University. Many friends and colleagues have offered me congratulations and I understand why. It is not because I have caused these events. He studied, passed examinations, asking professors' questions, and generally conducted himself in a manner that brings honor to his family and the university.

I am not being coy when I say that the best his parents, any parents, can do is to try and create a platform from which their children can influence their futures. There are no certain paths to success although we pretend that there is one. But there are people who prepared more faithfully than others only to suffer some great roadblock or even abject failure and not necessarily related to anything that they might have done.

To believe otherwise is to build your hopes on an always benevolent god who will ensure your success simply because you are a good person, committed no major sins or crimes, and just worked your ass off for a piece of the pie. Hello? Reality? Do you think that every starving person in Africa failed to do the proper things? Did all those who died before "their time" in these wars of liberation/ repression/ revenge?

But not to worry because if the M Theory proves true, then perhaps in one of the 11 parallel universes something is going right for them in one of them. Do not misunderstand my point. Parents are crucial to raising healthy children. But parents cannot cause their children to be failures or successes. Children contribute heavily to that mix.

Nevertheless, I am proud of his successes because I did contribute to them no matter the measure. It will be a good day when I see family members gathered to anoint this new man. I know he was a man before, but college graduation is a part of the maturation rituals that we must pass through. And for an African American male, passing through that portal is so regrettably rare.

I remember the first time I held him. He was just born, the doctor allowed me to cut the umbilical cord (but not really – she did the primary cut and I did a ceremonial cut that I was supposed to think was primary). I first told him his name. I then recited the adhan in his right ear and the iqamah in his left ear.

I felt a surge of energy from him to me that was absolutely intensely joyful. I felt a surge of energy later when his sister was born but, and bear with me, the energy from her was, well, painful. That really disturbed me. To think that my daughter was causing me some pain while my son caused this joy earlier was confounding. Later, I developed a theory that works for me.

My theory is that we're like magnets. Opposites attract, similarities repel. My son is more like his mother and my daughter is more like me. His mother is a physician; he'll be a physician. I make my living really as a technical writer and my daughter majors in journalism.

73. Monday, June 19, 2006

BUSH ADMINISTRATION TRIES TO BLOCK STATE'S PROBE
OF TELECOMS & NSA

CALMING ALONENESS
The calmness of aloneness fills my living spaces like the ten o'clock sun. It has been a month and a half since she left. I have not rued my decision not to protest her decision to leave. Perhaps she didn't want to be married at all. Only she knows and I can't see what good it would do me to know which it is.

A rancor-free environment restores sanity with the balm of reflection and meditation. Spiritual struggle is the most daunting when we our hearts and souls are fodder in the bonfire of egos.

Women appear differently now. When my wife and I were together, I still appreciated the visual satisfaction I derived from looking at attractive women. I was not looking at them lustfully because I was faithful to her even when she put me on restriction or extended fasts. These are not metaphors. But I remained committed to my vows until she left me. Since there is no possibility of reconciliation, subtly my interests in women began returning.

I sense the stirrings of a renascent passion, which for me means being in a sensuous and fiery relationship with a woman with whom I share other, non-lethal interests.

Odds and Ends
Finally, I'm going to get to see Ronaldinho play in person. Barcelona is coming to my hometown to play a match against Chivas of Guadalajara. I'd requested to be put on a speculative list and even placed my money where my mouth was. And now it is paying off. On a beautiful summer evening, I will see one of the finest players to ever grace the pitch.

The Americans awoke against the soccer giant Italy and drew. It was one of the poorest refereed matches I've seen. It is, after all, an integral part of the sport to roast the referees. However, for those of us who have worked as referees, we know that the fan sees basically very little of what happens on the pitch. Aggravating generally poor viewing is the public's general ignorance of the laws of the game. Even learning the language of the laws will not prepare a person to judge whether the referee's call was correct.

The announcing at the WC has been absolutely atrocious. For example, today a Spanish player tripped a Togo player in the box after the striker had beaten him with some amazing ball skills. The referee ignored the foul and the announcers said: Announcer #1: the referee isn't going to call for a penalty kick! Announcer #2: he isn't going to even call a foul!

Well, you see, the problem is that a foul by the defenders in the box will automatically result in a free kick from the penalty spot (hence: penalty area and penalty kick!). He should know that. They are not speaking the language of the sport. They are demonstrating their cultural arrogance with lame baseball analogies, incorrect terminology, too much personal background information, and most fatal of all, a complete ignorance of tactics and strategies.

One last example. Spain substituted a player at the start of the second half. This was a strategic move as Spain was trailing by a goal at that time. In Europe the announcer would have noted it and then would have suggested that the substitution was designed to increase the number of attacks, as the new player is a left footed attacking midfielder to give Cristiano Ronaldo better service. The announcer said was, "Hey, there is a substitution."

America will never be a soccer nation as it has no liking for something it has not created itself to meet the limitations of its citizens.

74. Thursday, June 22, 2006

REPORT: HAMAS AGREES TO RECOGNIZE ISRAEL

USA MNT PUNKED IN GERMANY
I arose early enough to see the USA Men's National Team get whooped by Ghana. It was a result to be expected. The Americans played the entire round poorly. Opening against the Czech Republic on their heels, obviously intimidated by the size and speed of their side. It was embarrassing to see Beasley and Donovan back away from the challenge as if they were afraid.

The Italy match was better although the central weakness, finishing, continued unabated. The referee did a poor job but that isn't why the Americans couldn't finish. Beasley and Donovan played better but that wasn't difficult to do.

Then there was Black Star rising. Donovan continued to be invisible. The expected result obtained.

The Americans had a 4 5 1 set which means they had 4 fullbacks, 5 midfielders and 1 forward. This is a rather defensive set. Couple this set with Bruce Arena's hesitancy to push forward and you have a side without any known finishers slowing the game down. If Beasley and Donovan have anything going for them it is their speed. The 4 5 1 set muffles it.

And why didn't Eddie Johnson play? He is a known finisher but Arena kept him on the bench except when they faced Italy.

Anyway, I'm looking forward to Argentina playing as well as Brazil.

75. Tuesday, June 27, 2006

PENTAGON ADMITS TO NEW SPYING OF STUDENT GROUPS

WOUND LICKING FEELS GREAT!
Hold on a minute, I'm still licking my wounds. Ah, there; that's better. Its good to lick wounds every now and then. When the spit dries, there's this shiny, protective shield that actually speeds the healing processes. Admittedly, I don't have many wounds and those that nag at me the most are generally self-inflicted.

Isn't that really the way it is for us? We are actually more responsible for our problems than we would like to admit. Most of my more recent problems are clearly associated with my own risky behavior and when one is prepared to take risks one should also be prepared to suffer the consequences if those risks do not pay out as one had hoped.

Licking one's wounds does sound, however, like it is self-indulgent. Then again, most of what I have been warned was indulgent behavior was really quite enjoyable. So, I'll lick on!

I've been watching as many World Cup games as possible. There have been some spectacularly poorly officiated matches. The only thing that has been more disappointing than the refereeing (I should acknowledge that I am a former referee) has been the announcing and screen management. The announcers are often transplants from other sports and not very good quick studies on the intricacies of the game (as required simply by the title).

Even ex professional players do not always have a grasp of the laws of the game and the history of their development, which informs the referee on how to apply them. I won't provide examples here because they are so numerous; it is hard to choose the best one.

The graphics often cover important parts of the pitch. As a viewer, I must attend to off ball activity so that I might watch opportunities evolve. They put these useless graphics upon the screen and I have to withhold opinions and speculations until the graphic is removed.

Too much non-soccer chatter is also a pain in the butt. I know what's going on in the world and I turn to soccer, in part, so I don't have to deal with it 24 7.

I'm surrendering my insistence of doing the cover art for my book. I'm just not that good of a graphic designer. I'm going to have to hire one. The choice is not a choice at all. I either publish a book that looks like a senior class project or I publish a book that looks like it belongs in a bookstore. I remember how influenced I was by the graphic designs on record albums. Although it seems ridiculous, the artwork did influence my purchasing decisions.

I'm thinking of retiring in 18 months. I have to do my due diligence in determining where I'm going to be and what will I be doing, other than traveling and writing. 18 months!

76. Wednesday, June 28, 2006

STUDY: ALL ELECTRONIC VOTING MACHINES VULNERABLE TO SOFTWARE ATTACKS

THIS IMAM WALKS INTO A BAR...
I heard rabbis, imams, and Christian clerics discussing the commonalities within the three Abrahamic faiths. Rather than rely on the usual explanations, these people displayed a courageous disregard for literalism. This really heartened me because, although I know better, I, too, fall to the easy cultural nationalism, xenophobia, etc that seems eventually to seduce all of us, to one degree or another.

Rather than focus on the externalities of the text, i.e., the words, these people focused on the common themes suggested by the words. This is a common device of Muslim exegetes of the Qur'an. They say that they are looking for the 'illa (the essential meaning) of a word, phrase, or verse.

For example, the Jews have the Torah, the Christians have Jesus, and the Muslims have the Qur'an. All of these equal the Word. It is easier to compare the mythic personalities of Moses, Jesus, and Muhammad. It is more mano a mano a mano. If we had a tournament to see which personality we prefer, would we have actually determined anything more than the fact that we are trapped in the cult of mythic personality.

Each Word (the Torah, Jesus, and the Qur'an) is clothed in the cultural identity of the human transmitter, the so-called messenger. Imagine the ineffectiveness of sending an Hebraic speaking messenger to China. What is important is not just the language barrier but what the language represents. Languages reflect cultural mores. When you learn a second language, you necessarily learn the codes associated with the words that supplement and clarify meanings.

The message must address the world of those who are to receive it.

And if there is "The God", why do we describe this god as "he" and as "supernatural" and as a remote, non-responsive clock maker? Is it that we are looking for god in all the wrong places?

I like the way the Qur'an addresses god's sexual identity. The Qur'an says, "Maa khalaqa" when it refers to the creative process that resulted in the male and female. This expression is often translated as "He created." but the fact is the gender is neutral as indicated by the unusual pronoun "maa". So the Qur'an is telling us... psst. If you pay attention, you'll learn that god is above sexual identity issues.

Now that we know that knowledgeable Muslims do not believe that god has a penis and all the stuff that comes with that so he doesn't have to prove to us that he can kick our feeble asses whenever.

But what about "supernatural" you might ask. I say that this is just some dated way of looking at the universe and we should stop saying this stupid word. I guess they had a view of their being nature and something other than nature which helped, I guess, account for miracles (the complex unexplained). But if this god is the only one able to create, then everything is natural.

In this naturalness, is it all possible that there is within us what the Muslims call "fitra" or our normative state? The fitra was endowed when, as the Qur'an reports, Allah asked mankind, "Am I not your Nourisher and Sustainer? And mankind said, yes! We bear witness." This moment, mankind embraced self-awareness and worship.

The light of revelation that appears both inwardly and outwardly activates the fitra. The outward revelation is the Qur'an. Inwardly, the revelation is tied to true self-awareness because the breath of god animates us and this breath is life itself.

Put down the supernatural and embrace the naturalness.

Enjoy the ride.

77. Friday, June 30, 2006

THE RETURN OF TUBERCULOSIS

BITS & BITCHES
SPORT AND PLAY
The earth seems to slow in its turns during the summer especially if you happen to be at work. The ocean is within a few miles; the bicycle is poised for a run. But the day is long and I am suffering.

The Tour de France is in a drug stupor. All of the top contenders, well, many of them, have been dropped by their teams as they are linked with the drug scandal in Spain. Doping continues to plague this sport.

The World Cup has taken some interesting turns. I saw Germany get by Argentina with shots from the mark after the closure of the overtime periods. The ESPN still doesn't get the problem with the graphics often hiding the players. That is so irritating! Then the announcers, even the retired professional player didn't add anything and they agreed on blunder.

During the second period, a player was fouled but the referee signaled "play on" motioning with his arms. The color commentator and ex-professional soccer player remarked that the referee did not call the foul. Well, in fact, he did. Referee's use the signal "play on" to acknowledge a foul and the advantage the team would have lost if he were to have stopped play. You'd think that Marcelo Balboa would have learned that by now.

WAR AND WAR
All of the dispatches from Iraq are still colored insurgent red. Afghanistan continues to build up casualties as if it's trying to catch up with its bigger brother, Iraq. I think Bush has an exit strategy: one soldier at a time, bagged and on ice. How hard is it for these men who have never suffered the battlefield to send so many young men to kill so many young men and the collateral damage of lives lost and maimed and forever shattered because... Bush thought Saddam had some weapons.

And let us not forget the wars that are not important to the price of oil or any other luxury item that we hear about only on a slow news day. For the people dying and suffering in these wars, every moment is newsworthy; every moment is cursed with the sound and smell of death and misery.

COOKING AND SHOPPING
I got my stroke, folks. I nearly cook everyday now. I'm enjoying shopping as I select various pastas, exotic fruits, wines, and fresh breads. I no longer overeat because it is in front of me. I no longer suffer through multiple days of the same grains and dried out fish because I was, like, you know, unimportant or something.

I still haven't completed furnishing the flat. I thought it best to wait. I've had to give time for the exorcism to take full affect. I've gotten rid of many of her ghosts surprisingly easily. As my routines settle, I'll expand my cooking skills.

LOVE AND LUST
I'd like to sign up for a little lust about right now. Love is out of the question. I'm still refurbishing the one recently returned. The best thing about it being returned was that I discovered that it had not been used. I don't think it was ever taken out of the box. I never would have known that had it not been returned in the original package.

My sensuality is returning after being blunted by the Great Bakersfield Cold Snap.

78.   Sunday, July 2, 2006

IRAQI SOLDIERS REFUSE DEPLOYMENT
ALONGSIDE U.S. TROOPS

I DREAMT NOT
The Los Angeles Times printed a story yesterday about a gang in East Los Angeles called the "Avenues" that hunts and kills African Americans, especially those participating in the regentrification of the neighborhoods within the avenues.

I know that I had experienced some problems but never anything like this. I've gotten unwelcoming stares and frowns but no one, except once in a bar, has attempted to hurt me. The bar thing? Well, this guy was showing off for his friend but I completely turned the situation to my advantage by disarming him with my wit and charm. I no longer fight. It is ridiculous. I regret having done it in the past although sometimes it did seem appropriate.

Today I faced a fear that I had let fester for more than two years. I was riding down Colorado Blvd. returning from the Rose Bowl. As I approached Figueroa, I began to break and to also relax. Oops. The front wheel hit an uneven piece of concrete and I crashed. Road rash all over my back and shoulders. My helmet disintegrated. The bike? Not a scratch on it.

So today, thanks to the Ice Cream Festival and the fireworks, I returned to the Rose Bowl. Not a single problem. I met two nice guys as I was refreshing my sweaty body (got excited, huh?) with the only decent beer there (Firestone). I do not drink Bud Light.

On the return, I came across a fawn standing on a small traffic island. I slowed and circled the fawn. It didn't take its eyes off of me but by her reaction, I knew she was accustomed to being near non-threatening humans. What a marvelous gift and invitation to return. The fawn eventually decided it was time to return to the woods above the Rose Bowl on a private road that I can show you one day if you could ever see your way to get on a bike again. You're still young. You've got two functional legs. I bet you're cute, too!

I've seen coyotes along the LA River and now deer at the Rose Bowl. You know, I spend time aboard Wind Dancer in Marina del Rey. There I see sea birds, jellyfish, occasionally even a small shark finds its way into the marina. But to see coyotes and deer in urban LA gives me a sense I can only describe as irrational hopefulness.

I think that I am making a new friend. I hope that it is so. By friend I mean, simply, friend. Right now, we're at the acquaintance phase. I hear everything she says. The prospect of making friends with someone who doesn't get the flag thing, who doesn't think worldly is evil, who seems open to whatever this thing is that occupies our waking moments.

Of course, there is always the dreaming way. I dream. I once heard that the dreaming way is the real way and the waking moments are illusory. Does this mean that my new friend-to-be is an illusion?

I dreamt not.

SMOKE FROM THE MACHINE

79.   Tuesday, July 4, 2006

CIA CLOSES UNIT FOCUSED ON CAPTURE OF BIN LADEN

BACK ON THE BIKE
Today, I was back on my 24-mile track that meanders from around York and 50th to Fletcher down the bike path through Griffith Park and back. The stretch along the Los Angeles River provides campsites for the nearly invisible homeless. The river is crowded with storm-freed trees, bent and brokenhearted Abrahams slouching toward Jerusalem.

Someone placed plastic animals, angels and saints atop sun-bleached rocks scattered in a little cove. It seemed oddly appropriate in a river named mother of the angels.

PASS IT ON
I saw a rider walking his bike near the LA zoo. When I inquired I learned that he had a flat and didn't have the tools or the knowledge to fix the flat. I learned as a recreational sailor that it is important for sailors to aid others when they are in distress. Something like that exists for cyclists although it is not as prevalent. That probably has to do with the differing environments. No one ever drowned because his or her tire went flat. On second thought, that might not be true. I can imagine a scenario. How does it go? For the want of a nail, a kingdom was lost. So, I fixed his flat. I asked whether he had ever helped anyone in a similar circumstance and he said no. Then I asked that he do just that. Next time he sees someone in need of a hand, he'll provide one.

MAKE NICE
I met a nice person the other evening. No. It wasn't like that. We talked and shared some. I must confess that I was happy that the place was a little loud because I got to look into her eyes closely as we spoke so that I could hear her. The eyes may or not be mirrors, but communication is improved when there are eyes explaining the words. I heard everything she said.

80. Thursday, July 6, 2006

WIKIPEDIA FOUNDER LAUNCHES POLITICAL SITE

EXPERIENCING CONTRARIES
This morning, iPod bumping, I walked to work in splendidly warm sunshine accompanying Bob Dylan on, "A Hard Rain's Gonna Fall". I struggled mightily to experience these contraries, audibly and visually. To paraphrase an American president: this was hard work. How hard was it, you ask? Impossibly difficult. This was similar to the conundrum of an unstoppable force meeting an immovable object, theoretically challenging but experientially impossible.

I have seen sun showers (rain and sun simultaneously). We then would say the devil is beating his wife. I have no idea where that phrase originated and what it meant or means. Some say it the rain represents her tears but why when the sun shines I have no idea. For us, it played with this unusual event. I also remember it raining on one side of the street.

The rain and sun phenomenon occurred rarely enough and it was never a hard rain, hardly rain at all, it was more a gentle shower.

Trying to hold these images (visual and audible) simultaneously led me to consider how this principle might apply to our relationships and us individually.

Considering this question on the individual's level is not that difficult unless we eliminate by rule obvious contraries (ex. being 100% English and 100% German). I'm getting a headache thinking about this one. The key may be to think of only objectively measurable contraries.

In relationships it may be just as difficult because nearly every dimension of a relationship is in a constant state of relativity. People tend to reflect the energy of the other in all relationships. When one person projects negativity, before long the other person will reflect that same energy.

What have we learned from this, boys and girls? I hope we've learned that contraries may not coexist in our objective reality but they flourish in our subjective states.

Sometimes those contraries are resolved by manipulating objective reality. The most dramatic (and for me, troubling) expression of this approach is the concept of transgender people. Troubling? Yes. Not in a judgmental way or in a way in which I argue the point with science or pseudoscience as referents. Rather, it is troubling because I can't imagine the angst and pain with which transgender people must live. It must have been impossibly difficult before the gay and lesbian movement helped by broadening the acceptable range of sexual expression for most of us.

WAITING
I habitually would wait for a woman to enter my life, which always put me in the hunter mode. Hunters always wait. A mat of leaves and twigs was probably prehistoric man's sofa as he waited for the game to appear.

But waiting for her to appear is not only the product of derangement it is also blatantly nonproductive. For one, if you are a man seeking a woman (one has to be clear these days) you must realize that women can sense a hunter better than any wild game you or your ancestors ever hunted. They are generally smarter than you and will not give you the opportunity to spring your trap. So relax and find another mode of behavior. Now, if you're a woman seeking a man, I have no advice because you already know that it is like taking candy from a sleeping baby.

I don't wait because this here dawg don't hunt. I am relaxed and displaying interest in the world although sometimes I display more interest than I actually have. In those instances, I do have to ask myself whether this is real or to impress because trying to impress is one of the early signs displayed by all hunters, especially the untried young ones.

I know what happens when I hunt. I've been remarkably successful as a hunter, which, at first blush, seems to be something I would brag about. The truth is that the most successful hunters are burdened with many memories of people damaged because they did not know the rules of the hunt or the subsequent feast. So it is really not a good thing for me to hunt.

81.   Friday, July 7, 2006

SHEIK URGES DEATH FOR NONOBSERVANT

REFLECTIONS ON FRESH FRIENDSHIPS
If this isn't your first time, I won't need to be gentle, will I? It is hard making friends in a city worshipful of automobiles and expansive lawns. It is difficult navigating the ethnic sensitivities and fears that percolate in all of our neighborhoods. I live in the Avenues. I didn't know until after I had signed the lease that the Avenues are the hunting grounds of a gang imaginatively called "The Avenues". Think of the creative energy being wasted by these knuckleheads. This is apparently a gang of Latinos that is dedicated to killing African American males seeking to regentrify their turf.

To imagine that there are enough African American males in the position to actually regentrify any part of any city reveals some important information about this gang and like-minded individuals. These guys must have the lowest self esteem observed among humans within the last two or three centuries. There are hardly enough African American males not in prison, employed with sufficient income and credit to purchase more than a spattering of houses in any neighborhood.

I think this attitude and its violent resolutions have more to do with prison culture and the expression of attacks and retaliations from the wars inside those walls. Anyway, I am striving to establish new friendships and that has proven as difficult as I imagined it would be. The central difficulty is that I prefer women as my friends and there are only, evidently, a small percentage of women who can comfortably handle the awkward demands of male friendship.

Their mates are doubly perplexed by the idea of their honeys enjoying a friendship with another male. They fear that their affections will be alienated. That is actually the legal term some have invoked when they sued their ex-partners for alienation of affection.

The problem is for the few of us who really like women (I think there are only a few because we are discouraged by women who eventually make sexual demands or their mates who think we do).

For some reason, I've always had women as friends and as lovers but friends never seem to become lovers and lovers never, at least very rarely, become friends. Being a lover is obviously not the same as being in a loving relationship. Lovers sometimes are more a manifestation of mutual sexual gratification (expressed in the most intimate and sensual manner) than they are of a functional friendship. Some think love deeper than friendship but I'm no fan of "deep" and I find friendships more sustainable and more fulfilling.

I have had a few lovers transition to friendship but the friendships did not really last and the mysteriousness of sensual-sexual dynamic permeated the transitioned friendship while it did. Nevertheless, always expect the best.

CATACLYSMIC MONDAYS
Cataclysmic as Mondays have become in the world of workers, Fridays are nearly revelatory. Fridays present workers with many options that must be telescoped into a few hours. To compensate people began planning their weekends days in advance or, in the case of an announced event, weeks or months in advance.

Mythically, Fridays are halcyon days tagged on the end of a brutal workweek that demands we spend minimally 11 hours in work or work related tasks daily. Consider this along with the fact that we spend roughly 8 hours sleeping, and 2 hours eating. That leaves us with 3 hours of leisure, at least on the days that we do not shop or run errands.

Let us guesstimate that Saturdays allow us approximately 8 hours sleeping; joy oh joy, no work; 3 hours running errands; and 3 hours cleaning and laundering, totaling 14 hours. We have ten hours to burn. That is triple our workday hours. So, we gotta plan.

This time distribution benefits only those who employ us. We may not be sweating but the long hours spent doing mundane tasks sets an unforgiving rhythm to our lives. Many of us pretend that our work is meaningful but the ants marching from sugar cookie crumbs to their nests are engaged more directly in their own survival. Our jobs increasingly have no intrinsic value but pay on the basis of our being able information managers.

Most of us are caught in the international web of finance and trade and none of us really seem to enjoy it that much. Besides, what Great Clock Maker in the Sky came up with this vision of fulfillment? Consider the amount of time we spend stumbling through the bullshit everyday.

Having the nicest toys on the block doesn't make it any better because, after all, they are just toys. And if toys are what it is really all about, then the Great Clock Maker in the Sky keeps a herd of reindeer and an elfin dormitory out back.

82. Monday, July 10, 2006

DEADLY HOMEBOYS MAKE A NEW HOME IN EL SALVADOR

MASTER GRAFENBERG? INDEED.
The World Cup reveals that international sports can be as ghettoized as American sports. The apotheosis of the Frenchman, in the eyes of some of the racists at least, is not Zinadine Zidane, Thierry Henry, Thuram, Vieira, or Makelele. I guess maybe they like Ribeiry but for all I know he might be French Algerian, too.

Reading a story in the Saturday New York Times about Zizou (as Zidane is affectionately called) that addressed the uproar in France over its multicultural team. Just as the ballers in every city, African-French ghetto bred kids, spend much time playing the sport hoping for a way out.

As we know from our experiences here, professional sports have very narrow gateways. Some of the African-French stars are trying to get the word out but when there are few openings in the wall, the squeeze is always on.

I was disappointed in Zizou's lapse against Italy when he head butted the Italian player. It was a sad ending to a spectacular career. The French were too old for the Italians. The better side prevailed. Age is a wicked taskmaster and no one escapes the scythe. Reap on, Mr. Grim.

The North Koreans add a morbid humor to international relations. They actually make the Bushies look reasonable and adept. This is probably their real danger. They lower the bar so low (how low, you ask?) that you'd have to be a mole to trip over it.

Israelis continue to kill Palestinians who continue to kill Israelis. Iraqis continue to kill other Iraqis. Africans kill Africans. Americans kill Americans. When you add these up, it is easy to see that we no longer need international wars to relieve our bloodlusts. Up close and personal seems to outweigh the popularity of our current travel abroad and shoot program.

If we can get beyond the mythic nature of belief in things unseen and acknowledge that the sciences (which are incredible) do not pretend to answer or provide much insight into our apparent need for mythic belief, perhaps we will see the ethical value of the stories we love to repeat.

As a matter of fact, seeing some of the photographs from the Hubble telescope rephrases the question of our role in the cosmos in a much humbler frame. How can we, tiny beings that live such short lives, be the crowning achievement of the Great Clock Master in the Sky? Doesn't this seem to reach the height of arrogance? So, I suggest that we all relax, enjoy the beauties that surround us, repair the ugly with your heartfelt love, and pass the word along that it is well.

When they ask, "What is well?" Tell them: yes. Let them puzzle, as you now puzzle, until they see what you will see.

I got a letter in the mail. In the letter, the writer said that I should change my name or adopt the title of Master Grafenberg. I really appreciate the compliment.

83. Tuesday, July 11, 2006

WHEN THE TIGERS ARE DOWN, FANS AND TEAM POP OUT THE RALLY CHEWS

HAMAS OR SAMAH?
I was watching a broadcast on the Palestinian organization called, "Hamas". I was impressed by it providing an array of social services to the people living in the refugee camps. I was equally appalled by its military actions that include the targeting of civilians. To justify these heinous crimes by pointing to equally barbaric acts of the Israeli army is to miss the point and the core strength of moral action. Attacking civilians should not be on the negotiating table; it simply shouldn't happen.

The historical relationship between Hamas and the Muslim Brotherhood is as clear as father to son. The principles of resistance to foreign domination using the core values of Islam is seductive to people who value both their cultural heritage and the maintenance of the same set of values.

When I looked up the definition of Hamas, it read: fanatic, fervent, etc. I then, completely on a hunch, looked up Samah (Hamas spelled backward) and it read: liberality, and other polar opposite terms to Hamas. Funny how that worked out.

I know how the Muslim Brotherhood is organized. It is a pretty well known organizational model that has been used previously in the war of liberation in Algeria, for example. It works like this. There is a small group of men, often five, called an "usra" or family. They meet regularly and study the Qur'an and other Islamic subjects. They also participate in group prayers and recitations frequently. Each usra collects funds to be used to support the most needy in the community.

Each usra has a responsible brother who is, in effect, its leader and contact to the organization through a brother who is also a member of another usra composed of brothers who have other brothers reporting to them. This pinnacles with the responsible brother for the entire brotherhood. This is a strong organizational model essentially because the members value it so highly.

The Islamic core values are well represented within this model and it is difficult for a Muslim to be introduced to an organization that demonstrates these core values in its mission and goals as well as its organizational structure.

However, models do not produce outcomes. People produce outcomes and many of the outcomes associated with Islamic movements have been ill conceived and mismanaged horribly. Hamas is a prime example. I know the core values taught by the Muslim Brotherhood. I also know how they are as easily corrupted, as the core values of the United States of America are corruptible.

We can wrap the flag around our sins but the bloodstains will still be visible. We can wrap the mantel of the warrior around our excesses but the hypocrisies will still be visible.

84. Wednesday, July 12, 2006

U.S. SHIFTS POLICY ON GENEVA CONVENTIONS: BOWING TO JUSTICES, ADMINISTRATION SAYS IT WILL APPLY TREATIES TO TERROR SUSPECTS

PRESIDENT BUSH:
THE "ALL HAT & NO CATTLE" RANCHER
When the public judges its elected representatives, it must consider the philosophical underpinnings of their actions and whether those actions were reflective of the public's ethos. It is not enough that representatives act expeditiously and efficiently. Rather, they must strive to act effectively and ethically in a world shrouded with dark motives and hollowed moralities.

Much of what the Bush administration uses to rationalize its foreign policy is the need to protect the interests of the State of Israel as well as the business interests of the Western world. These are not, on their face, malevolent positions. Whether the Balfour Declaration should have ever been issued is no longer the relevant question and the Arab Nation needs to invent another question. That Israel is a fact of modern life is irreversible. No human being should long for its destruction for to destroy it is to destroy lives that are no guiltier than you or I for the injustices perpetrated in its name.

Did not Bush relate the invasion and occupation of Iraq with the struggle for Palestine? Wasn't his success there going to clarify the Israeli – Palestinian struggle? Perhaps the Texas "all hat and no cattle rancher poser" president needs a posse to rescue his dumb ass.

AFGHANISTAN: highest poppy yield in years; drug trafficking reportedly financing the Taliban's resurgence in the south; warlords still running the country; central government not in control of provinces; border with Pakistan still very porous.

IRAQ: nascent civil war is ripping Baghdad apart; Shiite and Sunni militias committing atrocities against rival factions; Saddam's trial more and more the theatre of the absurd; oil rationing continues and domestic prices are skyrocketing; oil being diverted out of the pipelines into the black market; everyday coalition forces are taking losses.

MEANDERINGS

Very recently someone, on learning of the failure of my marriage, said that it should have been expected because it was clear to her that I had married beneath me. I was a little stunned. The comment was prefaced and footnoted with disclaimers such as non-elitism, but it really caused me to consider aspects of my relationship with others from a unique perspective.

Equally Yoked?

She mentioned something from the bible about being equally yoked. I didn't bother to look it up because I was familiar with the concept from the study of Islamic law that contains similar guidance. Muslims are warned that they should marry persons from similar backgrounds, as that will increase the likelihood of a successful marriage.

I thought about it for a longtime after the discussion ended but I don't think I improved on my initial reaction. The idea of class stability permeates all people whether rich, middle class, or poor. Each class recognizes its strengths and seeks to propagate that strength as it also rationalizes its current existence and worth. Today, especially among the mobi-centric middle class, there is much interaction among its ethnic components. Our increased mobility and elegant financial arrangements are quite distinct from the times in which those marriage laws and mores were coined.

I didn't marry beneath me although I do not think I valued fully our cultural differences. There were many superficial similarities in part derived from both of us being college educated that hid or distracted us from noticing the distinctions and their possible impact on our relationship.

85. Friday, July 14, 2006

HOUSE VOTES TO RENEW VOTING RIGHTS ACT

DOES GOD HAVE A JUMP SHOT?
When heroes and role models were gods, the gods were anything but divine, perfect beings. They lied, stole, and fornicated. There was always some kind of extreme and arbitrary punishments meted out to them by stronger gods. Those who followed their epic lives gained an understanding of applied imperfection that probably seemed more rational than the applied religions of today.

When we reduced the number of gods to one, we lost the option of having them behave badly or should I say, like humans. What would, after all, be the point of having a single god behaving badly? She'd be just like us and we know that no one should be praying to us.

I guess it must have been like "American Idol". I can see the gods rehearsing their powers in preparation for the inevitable showdown. Are singers in this season? Should I do stand-up?

By the time Jesus was selected, he had already died. None should blame him for the misadventures that resulted in his ascendancy. None certainly should blame him for the mythical nature of his biography; after all, it isn't an autobiography. But the problem of his selection persists.

Muslims are agitated by the lingering impact of his selection. It is not that they want the staff to go to Muhammad; rather, they have so depersonalized god that there is no longer room for divine role models whether they be the tarnished gods of the Greeks, Romans, and other pagans or the modernist perfected being of a carpenter's son. However, the attempt to make Jesus a heroic role model can only fail. He is bigger than life that means he is larger than the hero role and god as a role model is, simply, inadequate.

Now that heroes and role models have been recruited from professional athletes, we have partially reinvented the Greek and Roman gods but the need for perfection persists from the era of the god hero as one and divine.

People who accept their heroes and role models as flaw beings just as the earliest god heroes were understood will like Kobe Bryant more than most.

LISTEN TO THE BLUES
The Blues opens the door to a segment of our past that is easy to forget. You can start with anyone. You don't need a book listing the great Blues players. Just pick something up.

You could start with Son House. He'd give you a sense of rural people exchanging a hostile environment for a hopeful urban one knowing intuitively that the city was meant to grind them down in the name of someone else's wealth.

You could start with Robert Johnson and search for the crossroads if you're looking for a bargain on souls.

Or you could start with Keb Mo. He respects the traditions while forging ahead.

Everything begins with the Blues.

I THOUGHT ABOUT IT BUT THEN
I wanted to wail and moan about the horrors of the Israeli Army invading Lebanon, a nascent democracy unable to fend for itself or get the support of democracy loving nations like the USA (what was I thinking?).

I thought about ranting about Afghanistan and Iraq again. There is so much blood flowing everywhere. When do we learn to cry for the collateral damage? Have we built a monument to collateral damage? What would it look like? What if we made it look like the family of Latinos running across a yellow diamond shaped Yield Right of Way sign that we see on the California highways near the Mexican border?

I thought about questioning my fellow Americans about why we do not hear complaints about British and Australian citizens being in the United States without proper documentation.

I thought about asking my fellow Americans why we are spending so much emotional and political capital on undocumented workers when they represent only ½ of 1 percent of the workforce?

Then I thought more about it and realized the question was not fair. W.E.B. Dubois said that the problem of the twentieth century is the problem of the color line. The problem of the twenty first century is the problem of the color line. When all else fails, the world collapses around the issue of race.

SMOKE FROM THE MACHINE

86. Tuesday, July 18, 2006

U.S. & ISRAEL REJECT CALLS FOR CEASE FIRE

LACKAWANNA BLUES
Last night I watched HBO's "Lackawanna Blues". I had chosen not to watch it before with some conviction arising from a strange reaction to the word "Lackawanna". I can't explain it. There was something in the musicality of that word that somehow disparaged in my mind the second and most important term, "Blues".

Yet it does roll from the tongue sassily. It does beckon us to the rural past, our minds shuffling through the dust to the crossroads. There are always crossroads. Crossroads inevitably require that a decision be reached. Robert Frost challenged us to think about the road not taken.

The screenplay was well developed. The characters, by and large, were authentic although I think the period that the play purported to take place during seemed more evident of an earlier time. By the sixties, jitterbugging was passé and nightclubs and blind pigs were replacing juke joints. The Blues suffered the migratory challenges by fathering rhythm and blues as well as rock and roll.

In the context of Epatha's performance, these matters seem mere distractions. She was more than believable as Nanny. She was Nanny. Even when she aged, her eyes, the most likely betrayers, seemed old and wise. How does an actor achieve THAT? She must be quite a person.

It had a stellar cast. Beside S. Epatha Merkerson, there was Jeffrey Wright, Jimmy Smits, Terrence Dashon Howard, Rosie Perez, Marcus Carl Franklin, Louis Gossett, Jr., Delroy Lindo, Mos Def, Jeffrey Wright and Macy Gray. You can see from the cast, as well as the surprising executive producers Halle Berry and Vincent Cirrincione, that this production was a labor of love. Not one actor was there for the money; they were there for the art.

THE RELUCTANT JIHADIST

I have not heard of Vincent but it is good to see Halle Berry supporting good drama and making money, too. Ruben Santiago-Hudson, the playwright, is also in the movie but not as himself. Epatha is a very talented actor who also appears on a popular TV police series.

AIN'T NO MOUNTAIN HIGH ENOUGH

I turned on the television this morning to watch Floyd Landis recapture the yellow jersey in the oddest Tour de France seen in years. Here's a man with a deteriorating hip leading the pack (well he actually placed fourth on this stage but he does lead the pack overall) and posed to broaden his lead over Oscar because Landis is the superior climber. You may remember Landis as the one who left Armstrong's team because of differing philosophies.

Could it be that the tour is so unpredictable because of the increase in measures to prevent doping? It could be that the withdrawal of many of the favorites has resulted in an exciting if dizzying tour.

There are few, if any, people of color participating as riders in the tour. This is not a well-publicized sport in the United States. It is popular in certain regions and generally appeals to middle class people with the money, time, and predisposition to active use of leisure time. Road bikes are expensive to buy and not very comfortable to ride. You have to have more than an acceptance of pain; you must desire it.

A roadie requires paved roads. That eliminates many areas of the world. A roadie must have the time and materials to work out regularly. A roadie must have a bank account to purchase the newest, lightest, strongest frame, the best components, a good coach, and the wherewithal to travel to varying venues around the country and the world to ply the trade of a professional roadie.

I didn't come to cycling looking for a role model. I came to cycling because I've always felt liberated on a bike. I've always loved being outdoors. I can now afford obscenely expensive bicycles with outrageously priced componentry.

But when I'm tooling along the path and some little young whippersnappers come up on me and settle in front of me I am always tempted to accept the slipstream but my ego will let me snuggle for only a very few minutes. Inevitably, I jump out of the slipstream and blast by them with an expressive sprint. For example, last Saturday I was just kind of loafing on the path at about 16 MPH. I'm sort of daydreaming.

These people irritated me. They essentially crowded around me, one in front, one on the left side and one behind me. I put up with this nonsense for a few minutes. When I could see that the path was clear for at least a hundred yards, I swung out and went from 16 MPH to 25 MPH and I held it for what seemed like two minutes. Looking back finally, they were gone from view. I guess a little of it had to do with old man's pride.

87. Wednesday, July 19, 2006

ISRAEL BOMBS MILK, PHARMACEUTICAL FACTORIES, AID CONVOYS, CHURCH

DESPERATE HUSBAND

Sometimes one can smell desperation. It can shimmer like heat waves rising from too much sun on an asphalt road. Desperation can bead on the brow; it can soak your clothes in embarrassing places. Desperation is the antithesis of cool.

If I'm ever desperate, I know that I've lost my cool and need to recover it before the world's eyes thoroughly penetrate the persona that I've forged from suffering and joyfulness. Desperation should be a private affair.

When your heart is broken, when you feel abandoned, or even when you're actually the instigator – it doesn't really matter, it is difficult to move forward unperturbed.

I became desperate to formally end a failed relationship. It is not that the relationship's denouement was particularly colorful or stressful; rather, it was rather matter-of-fact. I think it is change itself that instigates desperate feelings. To bring this change to its crest, to begin to recover my pace is my true goal.

HE BLEW UP

Floyd Landis blew up while attacking another mountain. The Tour de France has been a little strange since it changed its name back from Tour de Lance. The Americans were hopeful that one of their better cyclists would continue to put an American imprint on this great bike race. George Hincapie was lauded as a possible successor although Lance equivocated when put on the spot about his old lieutenant's chances and who would know better than him?

There were a few others but the burden, at least recently, seemed to be all Landis'. But he blew up the second day in the Alps. Remember that this is the man whose hip is disintegrating as a result of a broken hip experienced during another race. He should not be ashamed or be vilified because who among us could have sustained such a torrid pace and with such a hip.

Failure is difficult to embrace, especially one experienced so publicly.

Now Floyd will have hip surgery and retire from professional cycling. Injury is the ubiquitous factor in every sport. The challenges found in sport always have the physical and the psychological components. Landis seems to have been able to handle the psychological struggle quite well as demonstrated by his awesome performance to date. But we can overcome our physical limitations for only so long.

88.   Friday, July 21, 2006

SENATE APPROVES VOTING ACTS RENEWAL

THE JOY OF SUFFERING
Suffering is the mantle that shrouds all our shoulders.

There is something oddly rewarding about suffering. The pugilist, picking himself off the mat, his face swollen and bloody, finds the strength to endure more suffering so that he might inflict enough pain and suffering on his opponent to overcome him. We roar our approval. We empathize with his intense and painful suffering in order that we might share the exquisite pay-off of his eventual victory. The pugilist goes on to become a legend.

I do not recall seeing a Christian church without the sign of definitive suffering that we all, Christian and others, knowingly call the cross, or even more specifically, the crucifix. It is also known as a rood. This is probably the best known symbol of suffering in the world. Its ubiquity has diminished its impact as an icon for all kinds of principled suffering. Must Jesus bare the cross alone? Of course not.

Muslims enjoy suffering during the fasting month of Ramadan. For the fast addresses our favorite human past times of eating, having sex, and talking about eating and having sex. We also enjoy ogling pretty girls, talking about pretty girls, and chatting up pretty girls on the premise that we have no premise; all of these vanities are to be voided during Ramadan which means Muslims suffer.

The Jews suffer because they couldn't keep their pact with Yahweh. They were given, supposedly anyway, this special, chosen status. Once they accepted it or acknowledged it, Yahweh started terrorizing them with all kinds of really torturous rules, regulations, and, to my mind at least, extreme punishments. Yahweh seems to enjoy the suffering of his intimates, especially the very special ones, you know, the chosen ones.

Everything that lives laments. This wise statement probably comes from some book of aphorisms or something. I first remember reading it as a song title on, I think, a Keith Jarrett album. And it is a truism. All that lives, suffers and dies.

Of course, there are innumerable kinds of suffering ranging from that which essentially entertains us such as sporting events to the suffering attendant to wars, famines, genocide, and individual acts of brutality and savagery. Even within this context, we equivocate. For example, we do not empathize with the suffering of our enemies; we relish it.

It seems odd but when we suffer, we enjoy it and actually credit it with making us better people but when our enemies suffer, we enjoy it because we think it will destroy them or at least deter them from even considering harming us.

Suffering is the cornerstone to music. Country music and the Blues would not exist, let alone be icons for American music, if Americans who created it (making the music and listening to the music) had not suffered, they would not have made that music.

A VOTRE SANTE
How much is your good health worth? I thought about this seriously because I had to decide recently how I was going to manage to feed myself. I didn't want to resume an old habit of eating in restaurants daily. There weren't really many choices after that decision.

So I began cooking. I've cooked in the past but that was primarily on the weekends that my kids spent with me and then only in a limited way. While I lived in Las Vegas, my "cooking" was pretty much heating frozen meals although occasionally I'd pull something a little more challenging together.

However, now I'm cooking true meals. Real rice (not that Uncle Ben's # minute stuff), real pastas, fresh fish (you gotta try Scottish Salmon Steak – use plenty of fresh lemon and a gentle rub of seasons is a good leader), and tons of fresh fruit and not enough vegetables although I'm getting better.

Cycling has taken care of the workout issues although I augment it with about 40 minutes of walking. I probably need to get another activity but I don't really feel it right now.

Sailing is an option except I am not inspired to take Wind Dancer out right now. I just mulled over whether to sell her since I've been basically a ground pounder for the past several years. Yet with retirement looming as a real possibility and the prospect of sailing the coastal waters still seductive, I've decided to keep it and not worry too much about restoration until its time to go sailing again.

A healthy person should have an intimate with whom to share another health promoting activity: lovemaking. I'm a healthy person who happens to be incomplete in that respect but there is hope. The fact that I'm healthy and active should increase the likelihood of meeting someone with similar goals.

LEBANON, PALESTINE, ISRAEL
There was this man from Nantucket who went to the Mid East on a junket, the wars were ongoing, the blood freely flowing, so he repacked his bag and said, "Fuck it!"

This represents how Bush responded to that area conflict when he became president. He undid what previous administrations had accomplished simply because of partisan politics. The region continues to boil and no one has an answer other than Bush's original, "Fuck it."

How do you get all of these complex intransigencies exorcised or at least mediated to the point where there is something agreed to that requires us to shape today together?

89. Monday, July 24, 2006

RICE ARRIVES IN BEIRUT; SAYS WAR
IS "BIRTH PANGS OF A NEW MIDDLE EAST"

U.S. SOLDIERS ORDERED
TO "KILL ALL MILITARY AGE MALES"

AN EMBARASSMENT OF RICHES
Driving home from Whole Foods, fresh fish, fruits, vegetables, and environmentally friendly cleaning products stuffed in my trunk while the air conditioning abated the unusually high temperatures accelerated by the monsoonal humidity, I had an epiphany: we, as residents of the United States, have absolutely no concept of the suffering our embarrassment of riches causes many nations to suffer. It is not as if we awoke one day and decided to support the exorbitant life style we enjoy at the expense of others. This is the world we were born to. Those who were not disconnected from reality were counted among the privileged controllers of wealth and a few nosy academicians.

The intractable Israeli – Palestinian wars, the wars in Iraq and Afghanistan, the "secret" wars in Africa, the massive immigration issues in North America: all of these and more are directly related to our embarrassment of riches. These are the costs associated with our callous greed. I have no idea of what it is to suffer intransigent neighbors with the fire and will powers to destroy my family, my community. And I have no idea of what it is to flee with hundreds of thousands to the uncertainty of life in a war torn nation as penniless refugees. I do get a little frustrated with the price of gasoline.

I have two residences. I have a nice car. I have three bicycles, two roadies and one just fun; I never seem to ride fun. Since my divorce (well, that is just signatures away), my health has remarkably improved. I've said it earlier, so this isn't a new thought: my return to health is not directly related to her decision to leave. I think the clarity of spirit that I experienced that allowed me to forgive others and myself for our mistakes, acts of meanness, cruelties, and betrayals also allowed me to live, as I should. I have a decent job and a little money in the bank. Everyday we ignore these truths because we feel powerless. We also feel fortunate to be on this side of the equation. An embarrassment of riches is a plague on two houses.

90. Friday, July 28, 2006

ISRAEL ADMITS TO DROPPING CLUSTER BOMBS

SOMETHING FOR THE BODY AND SOUL
Don't forget that this is the best time of year to enjoy free music in the parks and other outside venues. Lend the parks your ears and they will fill them with good vibrations.

I have yet to fully accept the turn for the better my health took. I am still armed with the analgesics and related items. The freedom that this improvement heralded is still blossoming in my imagination. The schedules and consideration I was forced to forge because of it are no longer required but I do have to remind myself of this daily. In time, I will become accustomed to my newfound freedom. This reminds me of the stories about the ex-convict who could not go from room to room if he had to cross a threshold because when he was in prison such movement required the permission of a guard.

Freedom Papers completed and ready to be filed. I love the smell of freedom papers in the morning. It's the smell of victory. You know, one day this thing is going to end.

SOMETHING FOR THE MIND AND BRAIN
The pattern of chronological thinking may be rooted in the brain as it sorts out the information it needs to survive. The chronology led to stories that led to the dimensions of backward and forward. The other confusing dimensions of up and down naturally occurred as well and probably related to survival in a less abstract way.

Now that we are, for all intents and purposes, trapped in our self-constructed time dimension, we will never grasp the universe from any other perspective. That is to say that it will take many, many generations to forge a new way of looking at the universe.

Through the double edge swords of language and mathematics, we have valiantly tried to conceptualize the universe. However, eventually we will have to admit that we do not have the tools to apprehend the world. We are limited to seeing and theorizing about the world based on our limited sensibilities and our brains inability to sort it all out.

M Theory, even in its incompleteness, does not let us avoid this awful fact. Are our minds able to form the questions? Are they able to grasp the questions? Will they be able to know when the answer is present?

91. Wednesday, August 2, 2006

SCIENTISTS: EPA OK'ING HARMFUL PESTICIDES UNDER INDUSTRY PRESSURE

A CALL FOR A NEW HOLIDAY
We'll need to hold a contest to pick the most appropriate name for this proposed holiday. So far, the one I've thought of just doesn't work: Freedom Papers Day.

Yesterday, dressed in the suit I was married in, I took the Gold Line from the Southwest Museum to Union Station, walked to 111 North Hill Street to petition the Los Angeles Superior Court to end my short-lived marriage. There were feelings of remorse and relief which is borne from task completion as the clerk reviewed my forms, stamped them, accepted my payment and bid me good bye.

This morning, my agent mailed the appropriate papers to my soon to be ex partner, completing phase two. There are five phases in total. I think the first one might have been more time consuming. But I'll reserve judgment until I'm all done.

I had the expected mixed emotions. The strongest emotion was relief. I am perhaps a little prematurely pleased with my ability to handle the marriage dissolution process without an attorney (the legal phrase is "pro per"). I say premature because there is always the possibility that a monkey wrench could get tossed into the works.

LAS VEGAS CALLING...
I spoke with a reporter from a Las Vegas newspaper investigating UNLV and its related foundations for malfeasance. The university through its related research foundation planned to scam the federal government by passing federal research funds through the research foundation to the university. The problem is that the foundation does not add any value to the research enterprise. Then why, you might ask, would the university bother?

The research foundation would charge the federal government for handling the funds and then pass the funds to the university, which would charge the university for handling the funds. This is not an unusual model. Generally speaking, research foundations manage grants and contracts for their related universities. All of the financial management occurs at the foundation while the faculty of the university conducts the research. These foundations earn the administrative overhead. This is actually a good model for larger research universities as the reporting requirements are substantial.

At UNLV, however, the research foundation does not manage any grants or contracts; everything is a simple pass through – no value added.

This mess started while I was director of the office of grants and contracts management at the university. We (my boss and his boss) counseled strongly against this model. That may have cost the boss' boss his job but there were other complicating factors as well.

All of this was driven by a desire to create a research-intensive university. There are many problems facing such an attempt in Las Vegas. This is the only city that I've ever lived in that has only one university. The academic and research enterprises are not highly valued in Sin City and the related businesses that generally support academia just are not there. For example, in Los Angeles it is not unusual for UCLA to cross-pollinate with USC in regard to faculty exchanges, and stealing researchers and support staff. There obviously could not be any local faculty exchanges. Any "stolen" faculty or staff was from another state. That is expensive.

That was one reason I went there. They offered pretty good money and relocation support.

A NEW MIDDLE EAST?
Now we know for certain that Bush is mad and that Condi Rice may have swallowed too much of his... philosophy. They plan to remake the region by supporting Israel's genocide against the Lebanese and Palestinians. No, we don't want a ceasefire until we are certain that

the ceasefire will cease the fire and until we are certain of the outcome we will continue killing whatever we find.

Okay. You're upset because you think as a Muslim I necessarily support Hezbollah. Wrong. I cannot support violence as a solution to violence. I do not understand the logic. Do floods prevent floods?

92. Friday, August 4, 2006

REPORT: NSA ASSISTING ISRAEL; NEO-CONS PUSHING "FOUR-FRONT" WAR

FROM THE HALLS OF HANOI TO THE SHORES OF TRIPOLI...
WE'LL FIGHT OUR COUNTRY'S BATTLE OVER LAND AND ON THE SEA...
Today the New York Times posted a story about a Vietnamese doctor who kept a diary during the Vietnam War in which she articulated her fears and concerns for her people and herself. The Diary of Dang Thuy Tran is a monstrous hit in Vietnam. One of the most telling impacts of the diary is on the Vietnamese youth. Some say that they now believe their parents' stories about the tremendous hardships they faced during the aerial bombardments of North Vietnam and the incredible firepower unleashed against Vietnamese whether North or South.

The diary will be available soon in translation for us who do not read Vietnamese. I intend to read it more as a cautionary tale. The wickedness of war needs to be recognized by all who moralize against evil. Many Americans supportive of the wars in Iraq, Afghanistan, Palestine, Lebanon need to sup on the fruit of their failed morality.

Like many Arabs and Muslims, I cannot help but cheer the valiant efforts of Hezbollah in its resistance to Israeli hegemony in the region. Ouch! Such a contradiction for me to cheer war for any reason after castigating my fellow Americans about their support of the Bush's administration commitment to redefining the political map of the region.

I am bothered by my apparent hypocrisy. If war is wicked, how can I support Hezbollah? In fact, I don't. Americans love underdogs. I'm an American who loves the underdog. I don't believe for a minute that if Hezbollah is successful the Lebanese will benefit from their benevolence; I don't trust them anymore than I trust that Israel will be a good neighbor – ever. I am not paying the real price (just taxes) for resisting the American – Israel conspiracy to redefine the region. It is too facile to cheer from here for any result.

I'll admit that I have no ideas how to bring peace to anywhere; I couldn't even manage to bring peace to my marriage so I cannot honestly claim in special expertise in conflict resolution.

The Los Angeles Times crossword puzzle for today, when solved, prompted me to reconsider whether my marriage was a failure. It reads, "In Hollywood, marriage is a success if it outlasts milk." Being lactose intolerant, milk might be the best yardstick for success since, in my case, it can be around for a little longer.

AAAH... A BRIEF RESPITE
Now that la ola de calor has all but ended, the evening breezes are welcomed guests in every corner of the city. Last night, as a matter of fact, I went to Old Pasadena to hear some music in the park but I had to leave early because it was too chilly. At least I was able to have two really outstanding mojitos made with real sugar cane.

I'd never seen it this hot in Los Angeles. It reminded me of my fated stay in Las Vegas. On one of my bike rides, my water was too hot to drink although I had frozen both bottles. If my legs touched the bike's frame, it was definitely unpleasantly hot. Fortunately, I know how to hydrate. I know how to rest in the shade when necessary. Normally on my rides, I don't stop. My regular ride is just 24 miles. Last Saturday, I stopped four times. Many were walking their bikes, which I think was not the best decision. They lost their coasting ability, which would have given them some rest.

93. Tuesday, August 8, 2006

PENTAGON: EVERY ARMY DIVISION IN VIETNAM COMMITTED WAR CRIMES

IN NEED OF IGNORANCE
When Genoese Cristoforo Colombo, AKA Don Cristobal Colon, AKA Christopher Columbus, set out to sea with a small fleet of leased boats, he was searching for a route to India in order to exploit its richest in the timeliest fashion possible. Although it is commonly believed that he was attempting to prove that the world was spherical, in fact, that was already established knowledge among the ruling classes of Europe, the knowledge brokers of the Middle East, and the East.

The so-called commoners of Europe still believed the world to be flat which, in part, accounts for the fear his crews felt when the fleet passed the Pillars of Hercules and sailed into the unchartered seas. He could not disabuse them of their ignorance and, as a matter of fact, he hid certain navigational instruments from his crew, as he feared their superstitions would lead them to rebel, take those instruments and attempt to return to the familiar. All of this is in his logbooks that have already been translated into English if you're curious about them.

The reason Don Colon became lost was he chose to follow the wrong scientists' calculations on the circumference of the planet; his group (and there were essentially two contending camps) underestimated it (I've forgotten why) and he bumped into a land whose northern reaches were, in fact, already known to travelers and explorers.

Years later, the more correct point of view prevailed but his error had already propagated misnomers (ex. aboriginals called "Indians") and a body of false knowledge that continued to influence the world for centuries.

We continue to nurture our ignorance everyday. One of my favorite examples is sunrise and sunset. We know that the sun is not actually rising but there are no cosmological words in our languages to address the phenomenon of our planet orbiting a nondescript star. Thus, linguistically, we are trapped in a world that does not exist but only appears to. What does this do to our forays into the unknown? Fortunately, the ruling classes understand the linguistic limits of our expressions.

Everyday, however, I encounter people who do not realize the dichotomy between how they express their relationship to reality and our knowledge of reality. Of course, the latter form of knowledge is too dynamic to integrate into the routines of life but it seems reasonable to ask why we refuse to even consider the impact of this dynamic on what we really know and how we hope to achieve a more honest relationship with the world.

Ignorance comforts us. I think we would rather feign ignorance for the sake of maintaining social relationships than challenge those around us to accept what we know for certain in search of some kind of negotiated reality. If we can lay our ignorance at the feet of those we hope know (or don't care as long as peace results), we can rest, however uneasily, and get up at sunrise and go to bed a few hours after it sets.

Physicists have been attempting to get us to see, for another example, how our concept of time is species bound and not at all related to how the world actually works. Einstein is simply a continuing force in this regard. The ruling classes have yet to distill his and subsequent findings that impeach our world views to the extent that even they, as theoretical propagators, do not fully grasp. The prime example today is M theory. I have a glimpse of its meanings and implications without fully grasping it.

I'll close with this example. Our appreciation of the world is expressed within the dimensions of time. For all of humanity, there is a concept of story that is based on backward and forward (i.e., once upon a time). Although we derive comfort from this, it is not a universal truth. Einstein spoke of a space-time continuum that, if considered carefully enough, impeaches our senses of before and after. Our physiological circumstances do not give us the tools to emotionally experience what we can prove intellectually. That divide continues to perplex us.

Ignorance has a place. But it is not the throne on which our trust should be seated.

Finally, I accept my ignorance as a condition of my humanity and at the same time I wrestle with it daily disturbing the cobwebby recesses of my brain and spirit. Knowledge has become such a broad enterprise that no single brain can contain even its indexes. Then there is only a kind of faith that can sustain me. A faith, not in a demiurge strolling through Eden looking for his or her handiwork, or a deity oiling his or her clockwork but in the ability to embrace ignorance as a permanent condition of being while pursuing knowledge, exoteric as well as esoteric; scientific as well as emotional. What I do not accept is facile faith systems or people without the spiritual tenacity to say: what the fuck is that?

94. Sunday, August 13, 2006

UN HUMAN RIGHTS COUNCIL CONDEMNS ISRAEL

FUTBOLISTA HEAVEN
I've been feasting on soccer lately. I sponsored a group of family and friends for the scrimmage (it was much less than what we futbolistas call a friendly – a competition that has no impact on league or any other competitive rankings) between FC Barcelona and Chivas de Guadalajara. I must admit my primary motivation, like others, was to see the great Brazilian footballer Ronaldinho live. I think most people were there to see him.

He didn't disappoint. For those of you who know football, you can appreciate him taking a high cross gently on his foot with the assuredness of Willie Mays shagging a fly ball in shallow centerfield. He was amazing.

Then days later I watched Barcelona dash the hopes of another Mexican club, America, that dared take a 4-1 lead into the second half. You know Ronaldinho led his team to score three goals in 10 minutes, leaving the match with another tie.

Please understand that Barcelona is only in preseason form. They are playing themselves into shape for La Liga. These exhibitions drew full houses across the nation.

I last saw them play DC United. The MLS is in mid season so one might expect a competitive match. Not. Barca outplayed them. It was embarrassing for the MLS. It demonstrated that the MLS is still a minor league with major league dreams. Barca's pace so outclassed DC United, that they were reduced to looking for mercy.

Some sportswriters would have us believe that soccer is not popular in America. The Barca tour proved otherwise. As long as these European clubs visit us and fill stadiums that hold up to 90,000 rabid futbolistas, we must ask that these pundits wake up and count the gate receipts.

If there were a league in America that could compete in the international market for players like Ronaldinho, I'd buy a season ticket in a heartbeat. And I wouldn't miss a game unless I was scheduled for a heart transplant that just couldn't be rescheduled.

95. Wednesday, August 16, 2006

SRI LANKA: CHILDREN LEGITIMATE TARGETS IN FIGHT WITH REBELS

GIVING MY LOVE TO PLACE LIKE THIS
I began writing this poem as an expression of the hopelessness that seems to define the relationship that I have with my reluctant neighbors. There is a profound sense of gloom that looms like the spray of death from the recently murdered. But I began to realize that this deathly smog is not meant for me but for them.

These people, my neighbors, seem to hate each other. They bicker hatefully over barking dogs, the use of a trash bin, anything really.

Many of their homes are fenced in signifying how unwelcome you are no matter who you are – they didn't build these fences for me.

Naively, I imagined a sense of solidarity existed among them but that is a superficial as speaking the same language. Even the children have learned this dance of hate.

I try to be positive but all of this is so unfathomable to me. The neighborhood of my youth wasn't idyllic but the neighbors were generally polite to each other. The neighborhoods where I raised my children were never characterized by such negative energy. And when I lived aboard Wind Dancer, my neighbors were probably the kindest. There is something in the sea, our eventual need for each other, which does not permit the arrogance of endless anger.

So, I deal with my daily heartbreak through poetry. I began to figure this place out as I figured the poem that had to come out. I usually don't do this but for you, who may be too young to get this, I have made references in this poem to the emptiness that characterizes the risen Christ (if he's gone, there's emptiness); lynchings, murders, and the redemptive nature of the blues, whether Jimi Hendrix or the defiance of Muddy Waters.

Finally, I ended with hope through forgiveness and love for which I thank Martin Luther King, Jr. and all of the other lovers who understood that, finally, there is nothing else that can sustain us.

BEING BOLD IN THE AVENUES
UAH 8/15/2006

I am a stranger in the land of my ancestors
Born here and kidnapped from there
Living among stooped refugees from hope's borderland
Who forlornly grasp risen possibilities barren as Golgotha

I am at once invisible and shunned
As an outlaw hanging from a poplar tree, feet dangling
Above the skulls and bones of dried fruit
Still sweetly enriching the burying grounds

Their red so confident, they flash
trophies of war and ribbons of euphoria

Their children glare, bemused puzzlement
Through tender cracks in the wall of silence
Their parents, piedra by piedra, built to deny
The death of dreams and my impertinent

Confidence striding by their tiny fenced in lots
Children's eyes, cold as grey steel barrels
Dirtied with the sooty residue of gunpowder
Follow laser beams to the warmth beating in my chest

My yellow in this case is not so mellow, in fact I'm trying to say its
frightened like me

Shattering the face in the mirror
I walk to work down a narrow path
Defined by the unfathomable
Wall of silence channeling the hatred of stones

I imagine their decayed houses, crowded
Dreams deferred in the stooping fields
Sliced by the razor wire at the border
Lost in the remnants of evacuated ghettos

And all these emotions of mine keep holding me
from giving my life to a rainbow like you

Still fiery hot with deathly fear
Prayers not answered, long distance pleas
For what is needed here if they are not to stoop
Again beneath god's cycloptic eye burning in the sky

I feign invisibility, listening to the Roots or Rakim
Spearhead quietly jamming their silence radio-free black man
Tumbling their wall, discoloring their smoking barrels with colors
As bold as love. Giving my love to places along the avenues

Because I'm ready, ready as anybody can be, I'm ready for you,
I hope you're ready for me

96.   Posted on: August 22, 2006 2:57 PM

PROTESTERS SEIZE 12 RADIO STATIONS IN OAXACA, MEXICO

WE NEED HEZBOLLAH IN NEW ORLEANS
Hezbollah has begun rebuilding Lebanon. Their crews are cleaning up debris and opening roads while simultaneously granting up to $150,000 to individuals and families for rebuilding their bombed out homes.

The victims of Hurricane Katrina, on the other hand, have not yet received funds for rebuilding that were promised more than a year ago. What does this say about America's resolve to help its citizens recover from this travesty dressed up like a disaster?

Do you think we could convince Hezbollah to come over here to help out those folks in New Orleans? At least they could show our government what a little love can do.

If this failure doesn't inflame the conspiracy theorists nothing will. As a matter of fact, I'm beginning to think there really is a conspiracy. How else can we account for the incredible delay in rebuilding the city? I think New Orleans doesn't want that old population back and Houston certainly wants them to get out of its environs.

Nobody wants the poor and unskilled. Maybe now they'll send them to Africa. I started to say back to Africa but that sounded a little like Afro-Zionism. And we can see where Zionism has led us.

The Israelis, obvious adherents to the policy of collective punishment, attempted to bomb Lebanon into the dark ages again under the premise of destroying Hezbollah. They failed miserably and at the cost of many lives, Lebanese and Israeli. But the true irony is the dispatch with which the Muslims responded after the ceasefire – did I say ceasefire? – that was to end the latest war.

Of course, Israel did not keep the ceasefire with Bush's approval. How deep does the hypocrisy go? It looks like all the way to the blackest regions of his heart. First, he encouraged Israel to violate the borders of a sovereign state. Then he continued his outlaw ways by encouraging them to collectively punish the Lebanese because Hezbollah had violated its border.

I saw a disappearing news report that claimed Bush knew of their plans prior to their execution.

Oh well.

I think we've sealed the deal on our family/ tribal reunion in Brackettville, Texas. Reservations (not a pun) are made for the flight and the motel. The name of the motel is the Fort Clark. That's the name of the fort where the Seminole Camp of my grandmother's birth.

Tony Warrior's kids were born in Mexico. Among them, was Juan Guerrero, our great-great grandfather who later became known as Sergeant John Ward, Medal of Honor winner, although his brothers continued to be known as Warriors, which is, of course, its translation from Spanish.

97.   Posted on: August 24, 2006 10:26 AM

U.S. JUDGE POSTPONES TRIAL OF ACTIVISTS ACCUSED OF ECO-SABOTAGE

DROWNING IN MY OWN TEARS
I thought I was ready for this. I had been waiting for it since I heard it was coming. Have you ever anticipated something to the degree that you knew exactly what it was and felt ready to visualize it only to have your socks blown off by actually seeing it?

Last night I watched Parts 1 and 2 of Spike Lee's documentary, "When the Levees Broke." It wasn't simply re-viewing the devastation; it was re-viewing the devastation in the context of other horrendous cataclysmic floods of New Orleans from the 1920s forward.

For example, I did not know that in the 1920s the government blew up the levees intentionally to direct the storm surge through the 9th Ward. For those with the racial chip on their shoulder, relax because at that time the 9th was predominantly white. It was a decision to protect the more upscale neighborhoods.

Realizing that many of the residents of the 9th Ward are descendants of the people who lived there then, or at least in New Orleans, it is not surprising that people believe the levees were intentionally blown this time. Our modern age is fraught with fear of conspiracies and conspiracy theorists ready to feed on that fear. Every catastrophic event can be explained by a conspiracy.

There was still much to learn from the documentary. The government was more than lax in its response at every level. It is interesting that the chief of Homeland Security was essentially unscathed by his failure to act and that Ole "Good Job" Brownie took the fall for everyone on the federal level.

Just as damning is the failure of the governor to bury her hatchet somewhere else besides Nagin's back. To be sure, he failed time and time again but she never forgave him apparently for backing her opposition in her run for the governorship. Where was the love for the people? Somewhere else.

I'm forgoing my scheduled bike ride to catch Parts 3 and 4 tonight. This has been a sobering moment in regard to how much faith one should place in any level of government.

SUCH A LONG DRINK OF WATER
Yesterday was Wilt Chamberlain's 70th birthday. Of course, he is dead now. Many people remain disturbed by his life story and many do not show him any respect. He was too great, too large to fit into our hearts. It was as if the creator gave him an unfair advantage over the rest of us but made him pay for it dearly.

Clearly, he was one of the greatest athletes in the history of competitive sports in the United States. No other professional basketball player has scored 100 points in a single game. No other player has grabbed 55 rebounds in a single game. In the 1968 season, he averaged 24.3 points per game, 23.8 rebounds per game and 8.3 assists per game. Hello? Can Michael Jordan, Earvin Buck Johnson, Larry Bird compare to that? Of course not. Yet he does not get his propers.

Like many my age, I am a little ashamed to admit that I preferred Bill Russell. Maybe because by all rights, Russell was the underdog who did relatively well against his nemesis. Russell was also a star in the political arena. He was outspoken and this was very important to us African Americans who had few true political heroes. For an African American to be so outspoken even while playing in a city marred by blatant racism is more than noteworthy, it was heroic.

But when it comes to just basketball, who are you going with? If you chose Russell over Chamberlain, I got Wilt and the game.

Once Chamberlain was front row center at a Don Rickles performance. For the youngsters among us, Rickles was the king of insults. They say during the show, Rickles essentially ignored his presence – until the very end when he is purported to have said,

"And you, you ought to be a ... high rise. Somebody ought to put a window in your ass." Chamberlain is reported to have laughed the loudest.

Admittedly, Wilt said some outlandish stuff, especially about his sexual prowess but we should forgive him that. Most men, especially when they were boys, have lied about conquests. The fact that his was so outrageous only speaks to how outrageous he had to be. If he were around, I'd wish him a happy birthday.

LOOKING FOR A HOME
Sometimes, not often really, I look around this country and I am so distressed at the level of poor governance, locally and nationally, that I just want to go away and be somewhere else. I am most embarrassed by our propensity to behave violently. While we wag our tongues and fingers at other nations and people, we support a government that is responsible for immense pain and suffering abroad. If we were to use the alphabet as a guide, we could begin with Afghanistan. So let's.

Do you realize that since the US government installed its puppet regime, Afghanistan has become the leading nation in the production of heroin? I wonder how much of that dope ends up in the veins of our youth.

All I have to do is spell it out, "Eye Rock" and you know what I mean. Or do you? Do you remember the years of sanctions that preceded the invasion? If you do your due diligence, historically speaking, you'll learn that the world was concerned that the sanctions were so severe that many children died from poor sanitary conditions and food shortages. The concept of collective punishment was not a novelty.

"I ran" is what every military aged person should do when the recruiters show up at high school or the local mall. Because Iran is Iraq's neighbor, all the Iranians have to do is look across the border to imagine their future. Hell, if I were an Iranian, I'd want some protection from those crazies squatting across the border, too. The one weapon they can understand is a Nu Cle Ar bomb as Bush would say.

Every citizen of the old Middle East must be trembling worrying about the Rice – Bush new Middle East. True that their latest gambit failed and the Muslim World is more robust today thanks to Hezbollah in Lebanon. Don't get me wrong, I'm not a Shi'a nor do I support violence but everybody has to admit that Israel got spanked. I know that they bombed and bombed but they lost the media war.

I'd like to find a place of quiet and reflection so that leaves out the Sudan although it is one of my favorite spots. Egypt is so weary and I'm so leery about the anti American sentiment there. I thought about Ghana. I know there are real challenges for ex-patriots. But I don't have a lot to stay here for anymore. Maybe a little closer to home like Costa Rica. We'll see.

I'm outa here. Peace.

98.   Posted on: August 24, 2006 4:46 PM

EU BLOCKS IMPORT OF U.S. RICE OVER GM FEARS

WALK THIS WAY
After living under the California sun for so long, even the gritty underbelly of urban blight has a pungency bordering on sweetness wafting through its neighborhoods. Its aroma infuses even the least of the houses lining slurry-covered avenues. Houses so distressed they seem abandoned except for that old man on the porch rummaging dutifully through a pile of refuse that seems to grow a little larger everyday, its odor echoing off houses across the street.

The sun eventually is taken for granted. The renewed sense of awakening, of being purposefully alive reflects off of abandoned cars streaming spider webs that have managed to entangle tiny leaves and iotas of dust. The cars' windows dulled with dust seemingly old as Vesuvius' anger.

And I walk this path no less than 20 times a week. I manage my way over roadside cement walkways that we all know as sidewalks, a very old shorthand indeed. They rise and fall precariously. Each cement square exists on its own. Fallen leaves snuggle in the cracks next to rotting flowers.

The one man who would speak to me has moved away. On his last day he introduced me to his wife and I then realized why he found me an oasis of hope in this spiritually arid place: his wife is African American. I have purposefully forgotten his name and hers as well. Why should I remember the escapees? All what we had in common they left behind. True, they did not move faraway. Nevertheless, the sole reason our eyes ever met was my traversing the roadside cement walkway that passed by their door.

I walk up the hill by the huge machines driven by men in hard hats. They are laying the foundation for a new dormitory. I have seen remarkable choreography of men and machines crowded together on a dirt stage. One huge machine ramming its giant corkscrew into the earth, then, pulling it up, each turn of the screw filled with soil reamed from the earth. It turns and shakes it off into a pile to be carted away by lesser machines we know as dump trucks.

When I pass the workers eating their lunch, they eye me suspiciously. I imagine them imagining a role for me in the world. Their eyes plead, "What are you doing here?" The black man driving a machine that carries things – I haven't a notion of its name – smiles and waves to me. He signals in our secret code that he digs my straw hat, and my style. I return the coded message with one that I know he will appreciate because it is consistent with our style. I know how to feign coolness even in the hottest times.

And we do this under the sun. For them, the sun is a nagging bitch, hot on their asses. For me, she is a momentary reminder that I am vulnerable but not endangered. I watch her nag them and I offer them little solace. I think about the time I spent in the classroom so I wouldn't have to bear their bullshit.

Anyway, that's how it goes today. That's where I am with this. Another day in paradise wiled away.

99. Posted on: August 25, 2006 1:50 PM

SCHOOL CHILDREN RAISE MORE FOR HURRICANE KATRINA THAN MAJOR CORPORATIONS

COLLECTIVE PUNISHMENT: A JEWISH TRADITION?
I know this is my second post of the day but I simply couldn't resist. We all recognize that the Israelis are very fond of collective punishments. They do it in Palestine regularly and their recent bombardment of Lebanon is another example.

Most of us, at least those in the Western world, are appalled by collective punishment as we feel that only the guilty should suffer for their transgressions. However, it is true that we all accept the phenomena of collateral damage. It is rather chilling to count the lives of people as collateral damage but that is the phrase of choice of our military whose job it is, after all, to make what we feel in our guts is unacceptable – that is, killing humans – more palatable. Thus, humans are classed as collateral if, by chance, they happened to be killed; oh, I meant damaged.

I like to read this serialized feature in Slate (an on-line magazine) called "Blogging the Bible". The author displays a wry sense of humor as he traverses the bible, offering his insights.

Today, he wrote about Moses and collective punishment. I've reproduced below, some really great stuff:

Chapter 31
Here is most hideous war crime in a Bible filled with them. As with the story of Dinah, it is sexual misbehavior that spurs the ugliest, evilest biblical vengeance. At the start of the chapter, God tells Moses he must complete one more task before he dies: taking vengeance against the Midianites. Why? For the fairly piddling crime described in Chapter 25. God was threatening punishment for Israelites who'd been whoring with Moabite women. At that very moment, an Israelite walked by the Tent of Meeting with his Midianite girlfriend. Phineas speared the couple to death. God, delighted by Phineas' zealotry, stops the plague he had sent against the Israelites as punishment for

their lechery. Even so, 24,000 Israelites die. For reasons I can't understand, God and Moses hold the entire Midianite nation responsible for this mess, and they want payback. If you ask me— and Moses didn't -- the Bible is willfully ignoring the obvious point. It was the Moabite women, not the Midianite women, who did the dreadful whoring that provoked God's rage and the plague. Going after the Midianites to punish a Moabite crime is as nonsensical as the United States invading Iraq to teach al-Qaida a lesson. (Oh, wait. We did that.)

Moses dispatches his army, which quickly kills the five Midianite kings and slaughters all the Midianite men. (This is not the war crime, but rather everyday policy.) The Israelites capture all the Midianite women and children and march them back to camp. Moses is furious that the Midianite women have been spared. (This chapter also fails to mention that Moses himself is married to a Midianite woman!) Moses orders his troops to execute all the Midianite boys and all the Midianite females except for the virgins. Isn't this a kind of sick, grotesquely disproportionate atrocity? It's collective punishment of a most repellent sort—and all to take revenge for the one bad date between an Israelite and a Midianite girl! Numbers informs us, with its usual fondness for precision, that 32,000 virgin females survive the mass execution (and were then enslaved, incidentally). By my rough estimate, this means the Israelites killed more than 60,000 captive, defenseless women and boys.

There you have it: collective punishment is an old, Jewish tradition. There is literally nothing new in the world, is there?

THE RELUCTANT JIHADIST

BETWEEN THE DEVIL AND THE DEEP BLUE SEA
UAH 8/25/06

Its New Orleans gumbo without okra
Daytime TV without Oprah
Liberace without the jewels
A black man without the Blues

Its morning without the bright
Crossed lovers without the fight
Elvis with no blue suede shoes
A black man without the Blues

Its pretty angels without haloes
Skyscrapers without the shadows
A crime detective without clues
A black man without the Blues

Its Dante's Inferno without the circles
Motown's best without the Miracles
A big L A lawyer who never sues
A black man without the Blues

It's the projects without the poor
It's Spain without the Moors
A carpenter's plane that never trues
A black man without the Blues

It's not the place he'll ever seek to be
Somewhere between the devil and the deep blue sea
A place not to choose, his soul he'd surely lose
Being a black man without the Blues

SMOKE FROM THE MACHINE

SMOKE FROM THE MACHINE

www.ingramcontent.com/pod-product-compliance
Lightning Source LLC
Chambersburg PA
CBHW022005160426
43197CB00007B/289